crEATe.

EATING, DESIGN AND FUTURE FOOD

THE FUTURE LABORATORY

gestalten

CO N TE NT.

PRE/
F/
AC/
E.

'This is a book about people as viewed through the lens of our eating designers, food products and rituals; the one thing it is not, is a cookbook.'

The way we eat and drink has always been a matter of taste, in every sense of the word. The food itself, its presentation and the social aspects of eating have always been strongly interconnected. But only recently has food been explored from a broader design perspective that addresses and questions issues of consciousness, traditionalism, functionality, recreation, the revival of craftsmanship and commercialisation.

Since the context in which food plays a vital role seems to be almost of gargantuan dimensions and infinite applications, **crEATe** as a sourcebook sheds light on those concrete new visual developments, trends and innovations that make a difference. In other words: the six chapters *'Food Activists'*, *'Wholehearted'*, *'Smart Food'*, *'Packaging'*, *'Food Spaces'*, *'Typologies'* and *'Future Solutions'* indicate how, where and why food is gaining new meaning in our lives and in top-notch contemporary design.

Based upon research from the London firm The Future Laboratory, the following pages detail the most current trends and data-based predictions through incisive texts, interviews and profiles accompanied by stunning visuals.

'Food Activists' starts by examining the uneven landscape of food and price politics with its environmental and production concerns, while *'Wholehearted'* goes on to address the return of the home-style way of both cooking and living (*'Grandmother's kitchen'*). The newest, most sophisticated choices being made around nutritional food and *'food as medicine'* are examined in *'Smart Food'*. The *'Packaging'* chapter introduces the new challenges we face in delivering high-impact aesthetic and brand experiences while remaining (or becoming) cost effective and sustainable. The concepts and interior design approaches of the *'Food Spaces'* section present the evolution of interiors where we eat and drink into luxurious canteens, cooking laboratories and shops. Our diverse attitudes in embracing food and how it creates identity (*'you are what you eat'*) are investigated and defined in *'Typologies'*. Finally, **crEATe** looks ahead with *'Future Solutions'* by illuminating emerging trends and illustrating how food will look, as well as how we will respond to it emotionally and aesthetically, in coming years.

All this is exemplified with striking photography featuring visuals from the fields of product, industrial and interior design to branding and consumerism. This is a book about people as viewed through the lens of our eating designers, food products and rituals; the one thing it is not, is a cookbook.

FO/ OD ACTI/ VISTS.

'Consumers are struck by the level of perplexity around food choices. They are getting so many conflicting messages from industry, science, government and journalism, that the landscape of food has become treacherous.'

_ Michael Pollan, author, In Defense of Food

POLITICS OF THE PLATE

Western consumers have come to expect cheap food. In the US, the proportion of income spent on food has halved from 20% in the 50s to 10% last year. Similar figures can be found in other developed nations. Foods once considered luxuries, such as salmon, steak and champagne, are now shopping basket regulars.

A global economic downturn coupled with the rising price of commodities due to climate change means that food is more of a political issue than ever before. The food divide is growing, not just between wealthy and developing nations, but also among social classes in Western countries. What we choose to eat has never said more about our political outlook than it does now.

Up, up and away

Long-established trading routes mean that most countries have not been self-sufficient in terms of food for many years. For a number of reasons, global food prices are currently rising. Increasingly, domestic food security worldwide is dependent on global prices. An increase in oil prices translates into higher harvest and freight costs while increased urbanisation means that most food has to be transported – according to UN figures, over 60% of the world's population will live in urban areas by 2030. In recent years, all the key wheat-producing nations, apart from the US, have experienced poor harvests as climate change brings unpredictable and unseasonal weather.

Throughout history, as nations have become richer they have consumed more meat – this is the nutrition transition. Today, we are seeing this happen in emerging (and populous) nations such as India and China. The 21st-century version of nutrition transition also places cachet on imported goods in general, as another way for people to demonstrate their status. The price of dairy has risen almost 65% in the past year, mainly due to changing appetites in China, where demand is increasing at around 25% annually. In fact, a third of all milk produced is now heading for China, a country with little internal dairy production. However, it is the diversion of crops from food to biofuels that could have the biggest impact on food prices. As well as rising prices of corn and grain-based food, the meat and dairy industries that rely on grain for feed will pass those increased costs onto the consumer.

Food riots

In the developing world, lower salaries mean that the impact of rising food prices is being felt acutely. Last year, tens of thousands marched through Mexico City's streets to protest a 400% rise in tortilla prices. Poor Haitians unable to afford rice and beans have been driven to eating 'terre', biscuits made of clay, water and shortening. The West is also beginning to feel the pinch. Last September, Italian consumer groups called a one-day 'pasta strike', urging consumers to boycott the national dish in the face of a 20% price hike. But the repercussions will also be felt in other countries: in the UK, pasta is such a regular in the shopping baskets of the population that it is included in the annual Consumer Prices Index (CPI).

Label mates

While price looks to be the issue that will be most resonant with consumers, the landscape that has evolved over the past five years also brings other concerns to the fore. Since the terms 'food miles', 'carbon footprint', 'Fairtrade' and 'organic' have

---

opposite | I-cakes by Martí Guixé, the pie graphic indicates the ingredients of the cake in percentages. **below from left** | 'Meat Factory' by Tithi Kutchamuch aims to promote respect for supermarket-sold meat; easy bean 'giving beans the culinary status they deserve', products are hand-prepared in small batches. Packaging and branding by Here Design.

entered common parlance, shoppers have even more informa-tion-saturation, controversies and politics to contend with.

Superfoods, plastic bags and obesity have become the stuff of newspaper headlines, while supermarket produce displays labels from a myriad of regulatory bodies. Take the organic debate. '*Sceptics believe the organic label to be nothing more than a marketing tool rather than a set of principles, and there are criti-cisms of some organic production on a grand scale,*' says Peter Norton, project manager at the Bulmer Foundation, a charity promoting sustainable development. '*And with the organic market growing at twice the rate of the conventional grocery market, there are concerns about meeting the need.*'

Indeed, we are buying organic in droves; in 2006, organic food and drink sales hit the £2bn mark. Yet we are increasingly confused about whether it is better for us. '*One week organic is better, and the next week it's something else,*' says a member of the LifeSigns Network, a global consumer group. Bulmer feels that more radical foodies will move to '*permaculture, land reform, and community land ownership*' as the organic movement becomes more mainstream. This provides some insight into the future direction of the green food movement.

Waist not, want not

Health is no longer a purely personal issue; it has moved into the public and moral arena. The World Health Organization predicts that by 2015, roughly 2.3bn adults worldwide will be overweight, and more than 700m will be obese; in other words, there will be an obesity epidemic. Suddenly fat will become a political issue.

The European Union has moved to make standardised food labelling compulsory across all member countries. Labels should display sugar, salt, fat, saturated fat and carbohydrate content. In Italy, poor lifestyle is implicated in 90% of deaths to the point that the Italian government has created an action plan that includes reducing the price of fresh fruit and vegetables, introducing produce into hospitals, schools and offices, and increasing health education in schools.

However, some commentators are taking a far more hardline stance. In a US trial, obese adults were offered $14 for every 1% reduction in their body weight. In Mississippi, representatives have introduced a bill that prohibits food establishments '*from serving food to any person who is obese.*' Australian nutritionist Dr John Tickell has urged the country's airlines to treat the

excess fat on obese passengers as excess baggage and charge them extra for it. While the last two examples have not been included in legislation (yet), the fact that they are subjects for open discussion underlines an increasing hostility towards the overweight.

On the other hand, fat people are fighting back. We've seen the growth of the Fatosphere blogging community, which features contributors such as The Rotund, Fat Chicks Rule, Fatgrrl and Big Fat Deal. In an interview, Kate Harding, founder of the Shapely Prose blog, said: '*What we're saying is that exercise and a balanced diet do not make everyone thin.*'

---

below | Belu carbon neutral bottled water in compostable packaging.
opposite clockwise from above | wilderness gourmet course by Dryad Bushcraft, Swansea; VG Burgers, Organic Fast food in Boulder, Colorado; Fortnum & Mason honey made by bees living on the roof of the London Piccadilly store; Wild Bunch & Co cold-pressed organic juice.

_'Sceptics believe the organic label to be nothing more than a marketing tool rather than a set of principles, and there are criticisms of some organic produc-tion on a grand scale.'

Greenhouse gases

The next area for green campaigners to explore in the public arena will be the environmental impact caused by food production, including deforestation. On this battlefield, vegetarians can prepare to take the moral high ground, as scientists single out reducing meat consumption as a way to cut emissions. *'The environmental issues in meat eating are very serious, and meat eating is very unsustainable. It becomes more sustainable if we do it well and use it all,'* notes Michael Pollan, author and professor of science and environmental journalism at UC Berkeley. Global agricultural industry accounts for a fifth of greenhouse gases, with livestock accounting for a high proportion of this.

Thought for food

Food documentaries have shifted from singling out and exposing the unhealthy food and practices of the fast food industry (Super Size Me, McLibel, Fast Food Nation) to investigating the food production industry as a whole, bringing yet more issues to the public's attention. Darwin's Nightmare concerns the fishing industry in Tanzania, where Nile perch fillets are flown to European markets while locals make use of the discarded skeletons. Black Gold aims to highlight the injustice of a world where cappuccinos cost £3 and yet coffee growers are impoverished. Sharkwater uncovers the illegal finning industry that provides shark fin soup. Our Daily Bread shows impersonal and industrial methods of food production in vivid detail.

POSITIVE PURCHASING

While consumers feel largely powerless to stop climate change, they are voting with their pocketbooks and choosing products that have a positive impact on the environment and their fellow humans.

Slow down

In Europe and America, the Slow Food movement has increasing power over what we eat. *'Slow Food believes in the philosophy of good, clean and fair,'* says a spokeswoman. *'These concepts relate to food in all its forms, from the ground to the table.'* There are 86,000 members of the Slow Food movement worldwide with offices in Italy, Germany, Switzerland, the US, France, Japan and the UK. In his book In Defense of Food, Michael Pollan extols the virtues of real food over processed. *'When you process foods, they lose not only nutrition, but taste, and that's why you have to fill them with fat, salt and sugar,'* says Pollan. *'You're making up for something that's been lost.'*

Inverted quarantine

However in America, we are seeing self-preservation as a driver of healthier eating. In his book Shopping our Way to Safety: How we Changed from Protecting the Environment to Protecting Ourselves, Andrew Szasz identifies the *'inverted quarantine'* phenomenon. Consumers are isolating themselves and their families from the perceived danger of their local environment by buying into organic, filtered water and natural goods. Using their power as consumers, they are acting to protect the individual.

Animal welfare

But it's not just the individual or the environment that those with purchasing power are electing to preserve. They are also concerned about the animal they will be eating. *'Consumers do want to know more, they want to know how their animal is reared,'* says Leigh Grant, chief executive of Freedom Food, an RSPCA-sponsored animal welfare scheme. According to a survey by UK supermarket Co-op, Britons are more concerned about animal welfare and fair trade than climate change. Just 4% of the 100,000-strong sample rated climate change their top priority, compared to 25% who supported better animal welfare and 27% who prioritised ethical trading. In response to these findings, the supermarket chain has removed all caged hen products from its shelves and is converting its entire hot drinks range (tea, coffee, hot chocolate) to Fairtrade. The making of foie gras, where geese are force-fed to change the consistency of their livers, has long been considered a cruel practice. Chicago was the first city in the world to ban the sale of foie gras, and is likely to be followed by the state of California and the English city of York.

right | LOCAL RIVER by Mathieu Lehanneur is a home storage unit for fish and greens. This project aims to reduce impact on the environment by the transport of foodstuffs, while ensuring their traceability. **opposite** | *'my sweets'* by Tithi Kutchamuch addresses issues such as overeating, eating disorders, obesity, illness, guilt and food waste.

RETHINKING PRICE

In western society, consumers aged below 50 have never experienced food inflation. Energy-inefficient, centralised food supply systems will become too expensive to maintain. But the good news is that paying more for food could mean that consumers rethink its real value.

Food metres

Consumers are increasingly worried about the '*carbon footprint*' of transporting the contents of their shopping trolley. Grapes from Egypt, basil from Israel and green beans from Kenya are favoured over British and European produce by supermarkets. In response to shoppers' concerns, Tesco is developing a label that will map the carbon footprint of products, including tomatoes and orange juice. Local food has been positioned as an environmentally friendly alternative by green campaigners, not only because it is transported shorter distances but also because it promotes biodiversity. If the growing cost of transporting food is passed on to customers, will local become even more appealing?

Some shoppers are already actively trying to buy local. '*The local food, farmers' market and community-supported agriculture movements have done an amazing job considering the odds they're up against,*' says Alex Steffen, executive editor of Worldchanging. In the US, LocalHarvest uses a Google Maps mash-up to show local farmers' markets, farms, organic restaurants and co-operative grocery stores. A study by the New Economics Foundation think-tank found that every £10 spent locally is worth £25 to the local community, while the same money spent in a supermarket is worth only £14 to that economy. '*Local has captured the public imagination and people want to know the provenance of their food,*' says Peter Norton of the Bulmer Foundation. '*But, of course, local doesn't necessarily mean responsible.*'

Clocked mileage: local vs. cargo

A growing number of academics believe that food miles are not the only consideration. The energy consumed in food production is now on the radar. Researchers at New Zealand's Lincoln University found that, taking into account factors such as harvesting techniques, fertilizer and water use and renewable energy applications, New Zealand lamb produced 1,520 pounds of CO_2 emissions per ton to British lamb's 6,280 pounds. This may seem surprising, but New Zealand lambs are raised almost solely on pastures, whereas the British lambs' diet is supplemented by feed, which has its own carbon cost.

Because of the freight of imports, the French wine industry has come under attack from cheaper New World imports. Now some French vineyard owners are fighting back by making the transit of their wines greener. For example, 60,000 bottles of wine will be shipped from Languedoc to Ireland in a 19th-century sailing ship. The process will take a week longer than airfreight but will save almost 5 ounces of carbon per bottle. Ships will return to France full of empty bottles for recycling. It is a solution that makes one wonder: Why don't brands think about transporting items by barge using canal networks rather than by road?

Home cooking and bargain shopping

Ernst & Young reports that, after taxes and bills are paid, the average household has only 22% of its income left, down from 28% in 2003. As recession looms, we expect that consumers will tighten their belts. Currently, Americans spend approximately half of their overall food budget on eating out. '*Eating out means that people have become more adventurous in their tastes,*' says Leigh Grant of Freedom Food. '*They are much more likely to try something new. I believe people will eat out less, but want to maintain better quality in what they cook at home.*' To do this, a generation of affluent shoppers in Europe is turning to discount superstores such Netto, Aldi and Lidl, where the quality of food is deceptively high. These discount shoppers are confident enough in their tastes to not need to hide behind expensive brand names.

Food insecurity and urban farmers

In a sign of the extremity, consumers are beginning to take matters into their own hands by producing their own food. UN Development Programme researchers have found herbs growing on rooftops in Santiago, cacti in Mexico City and pigeons kept in Cairo.

To reduce the distance food travels and increase the self-sufficiency of cities, it will be imperative that land is earmarked for food production before and as cities expand. In Shanghai, one of the world's fastest growing cities, consultancy firm Arup is co-planning a satellite eco-city, Dongtan, to accommodate the incoming population. The city will feature waste management recycling, natural wetlands and will spread the population out to maximise energy efficiency.

Vertical farming

'*We do a lot to protect ourselves from the elements, but nothing to protect our food,*' says Dr Dickson Despommier, professor of environmental health sciences at New York's Columbia University. Despommier and his staff have suggested '*vertical farming*' as a solution to the food production problems envisaged by reports such as the UN's Food and Agriculture Organization's '*State of Food Insecurity in the World*', which looks at how changing weather and distribution networks are affecting world hunger. Vertical farming would involve custom-built high-rises in cities that contain indoor farms capable of providing for the local area and beyond. Using sophisticated agriculture techniques such as hydroponics would mean shorter growing cycles and increased output. '*In a vertical farm you can grow crops in ideal conditions, which never happens in nature,*' says Despommier. '*Provide the exact conditions that the plant needs and it will perform perfectly.*'

Kerbside cuisine

Taking the wild food trend to the extreme, Arthur Boyt proof that this category of food activists is not the exclusive preserve of the wealthy. The former civil servant, now a cookbook author, gathers roadkill such as hedgehog, badger, squirrel and rabbit and makes casseroles, sandwiches, pot roasts and pasta. St John restaurant in London also serves squirrel, showing that perceptions of what is edible are changing.

above | The OrtaWater – Mobile Intervention Unit / Urban Intervention Unit consists of a diminutive 50 Piaggio, steel structure, 15 Life Line jackets, nine buckets and eight copper taps   **below right** | A place setting from the Ortas' 70 x 7 The Meal, Act XXVII Medical Foundation for the Care of Victims of Torture, an installation for 99 guests at Albion Gallery, London for which the pair invited seven artists, including: Reza Aramesh, Xu Bing, Shilpa Gupta, Kendell Geers, Lucy + Jorge Orta, Rashid Rana and Avishek Sen, to design an edition of 100 Royal Limoges porcelain plates.   **below left** | Lucy and Jorge Orta's assemblage of steel structure, shopping caddie, freezer, hot plate, ustensils, jam jars, and buckets added up to a concept for a small business that they dubbed a Hortirecycling Enterprise, Act II, Processing Unit.

FOOD ACTIVISTS : FUTUREFARMERS

Lunchbox laboratory

Design firm Futurefarmers' installations often involve nothing much more complicated than string, cardboard, wood, soil and, say, lemon trees. Their Botanical Gameboy was an effort to power a Gameboy by '*harvesting*' the energy produced by nine lemon trees. Typical of Futurefarmers is also their Lunchbox Laboratory, a collaboration with the Biological Sciences Team of the US National Renewable Energy Lab. Scientists have proven that algae, which can produce hydrogen and biodiesel, could be a viable form of renewable energy. The problem now is to find the most productive strains of algae among millions of strains. Listed under the heading '*Art*' on the FF website, Lunchbox Lab is a concept that proposes using school children as technicians to do primary screenings of algae strains. While Lunchbox lets kids participate in real science and network with other kids across the country who are doing the same thing, it

would also effectively eliminate non-productive strains and enable professional labs to focus on those most likely to prove useful.

Since 1995, from Basel to Bristol, Malmö to Manhattan and Riga to Rotterdam, San Francisco-based Futurefarmers has served as an interdisciplinary design studio creating new media, art and design for clients such as Hewlett Packard, Levi's, Nike, LucasFilm, Greenpeace and PBS. They investigate new media technologies, renewable energy sources, and '*new configurations of learning*'. Although they collaborate promiscuously (and maintain a fruitful Artist in Residence program), Futurefarmers, at its core, is: founder Amy Franceschini (an artist and educator) who also established sister studio Free Soil in 2002; Hamburg-based Sascha Merg (game programmer and developer); interaction designer Josh On; Michael Swaine, inventor and multimedia designer; as well as Geoff Morris, a design consultant, web developer and project manager specialising in human/computer interaction, and focusing on computer music and the cognitive applications of virtual reality. Not surprisingly, team members can produce anything from interactive installations, exhibition and book design to animation, 3D character development, and whatever you want in PHP, C or MSQL. What can't they do?

A series of '*sculpture*' projects includes a shovel that doubles as a pogo stick and their Photosynthesis Robot, '*a three-dimensional sketch*' in wood, foam, paper, thread and plants, of a perpetual-motion machine that derives its energy through phototropism, the movement of plants towards the direction of the sun.

Futurefarmers' Rainwater Harvester / Greywater System Feedback loop is a water-collecting system made from salvaged wood, PVC, rope, bicycle wheels and ... mint. Water is stored in three tanks that double as seating while variable drains allow users to decide whether to send the captured water back into storage, into the garden or out to join the municipal water supply. Pioneers in melding the virtual and the vegetal, Futurefarmers suggest that there might be no limits to the use of technology in making the world a better place.

opposite from above | The Victory Gardens Seed Library, was a series of lasercut boxes divided by microclimate that contained vials of seeds; the Rainwater Harvester / Greywater System Feedback loop is a water-collecting system that doubles as seating. clockwise from above | A tricycle suited to the severe hills of San Francisco; Lunchbox Laboratory is a concept that lets kid-scientists screen algae samples, saving biodiesel researchers time and money; Futurefarmers' Seed Friend installation featured seed packets displayed in a gallery for visitors to take home in order to save seeds from food they eat.

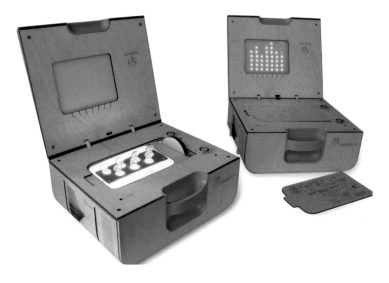

I. SENSES

Smell – Why don't we smell our food anymore? | **Taste** – Do you taste differently when the food has a different temperature? | **See** – Why don't we like blue tomatoes? **Sound** – Are potato-crisps still enjoyable when they sound like jelly? **Feeling** – Is an unglazed mug comfortable to drink from?

_from the eight points Marije Vogelzang uses to describe her own work

Commissioned by a pediatric clinic in New York City's impoverished Bronx borough, Dutch product designer Marije Vogelzang recruited the senses to tell kids who'd grown up eating fast, fried foods what should be eaten instead: '*I tried to tackle the negative feelings these children have towards food,*' the designer explains, '*to make food using Leonardo da Vinci's colour philosophy.*' Indeed, she used colour to cast the usually bland conversation about good food and bad food in kid-friendly terms, associating the hue of each food or wrapper with an outcome. Text on a green package suggested that green food would make the consumer rich, red was associated with energy and yellow with making friends.

The most immediate of eight areas of inquiry touched upon by Vogelzang's work is surely the senses. This is because, rare in the world of product design, Vogelzang's material of choice is food. She works with chefs as master craftsmen, just as another product designer might work with a plastics expert to develop a new chair. And, at 30, Vogelzang is the creative mind behind Netherlands-based Proef. Meaning both '*to taste*' and '*to test*' in Dutch, Proef is a four-year-old eatery in Rotterdam that serves seasonal, organic and local foods for breakfast, lunch and high tea. At its Amsterdam location, the staff keeps its own hens (Arianne, Anastasia and Elena) and grows much of its own produce. It is also, most importantly, a laboratory.

right | For Vogelzang's graduation from the Design Academy Eindhoven, she created an all-white funeral reception, including an all-white banquet.

II. CHEMISTRY

Dietary Science – What happens when food enters your body? | **Cooking Processes** – How was mayonnaise discovered and by whom? | **Kweekvlees???** – A genetically created meat (not modified, created), also known as in vitro meat, or meat made from the stem cells of animals. | **The physical and emotional reactions to food** – Medical Food - Allergies - Obesity | **Vitamins** – What do vitamins look like?

'*There is no other material a designer can work with that is so close to the human body and soul as the material of food,*' Vogelzang says. After only four years in business, Proef already counts among its clients a marquee of creative giants: Ilse Crawford and Droog, Hermès, Nike, Phillips and the Van Gogh Museum. On one summer day, the team worked on an event for a group of senior citizens and another for lingerie designer Marlies Dekkers.

Born in the eastern Netherlands, Vogelzang graduated with a degree in textiles from the Design Academy Eindhoven in 2000 with a thesis project that featured an all-white funeral banquet. Already noted by Droog co-founder Gijs Bakker for this piece, she went to work briefly for the school's chairperson and trend forecaster, Li Edelkoort and then industrial designer Hella Jongerius at JongeriusLab. Her business partnership with Piet Hekker, owner of Rotterdam's De Bakkerswinkel bakeries, began at Jurgen Bey's 2003 wedding where she created the reception dinner. The next fall, Proef Rotterdam opened, followed, a year and a half later, by the debut of the Westergasfabriek lab in a timber-framed former factory with a spare but cosy interior designed by Onno Donkers and surrounded by public parkland.

At every scale, and whether for corporations or non-profits, Vogelzang's work emphasises the context of eating, addressing not just the psychological, but the (al)chemical, technical, social and societal implications of food. Sometimes she works on projects of broad, global concern; at other times, she fashions a cocktail ring out of a carrot for her young daughter's lunch or improves quality of life for a handful of people in the most whimsical way: '*Thinking about all these people with fake teeth,*' Vogelzang wrote in a March 8, 2008 blog entry, '*I decided to make a toothless candy box. Filled with candies you don't need your teeth for. Sugary? What the heck, you don't have teeth anymore anyway! Imagine taking a moment to yourself. Slipping into* something comfortable (a flowery bathrobe perhaps?). Having a lie down on the couch and taking out your teeth. Opening the box of assorted sweets and enjoying things that melt on your tongue, are powdery, fluffy, liquid ...'*

III. CULTURE

ETIQUETTE

Communication – Can food bring people together? | **Culinary History** – Why did Roman emperor Nero eat so many leeks? | **Extinct Tastes** – Who knows how to prepare pig's head? | **Rituals** – Why do we eat a slice of sponge cake after a funeral?

CULTURAL DIFFERENCES

Religious Food-Laws – How do I know whether my food is halal? | **Taste-Flattening** – Why do children prefer Heinz tomato ketchup?

Many Proef projects are masterfully choreographed performances, in which the audience participates to complete the design through the very individual experiences each has. For a 2005 Christmas dinner for Droog, Vogelzang famously pared a meal down to one of its most fundamental rituals: the sharing of food among equals. She turned the tablecloth into a garment not for the table but for the diners. Suspended perpendicular to the table from the ceiling, with apertures for the head and hands of each person, the linen formed an intimate interior that contained the dinner party while obscuring what each person was wearing, rendering unimportant any sign of social hierarchy. For the first course, a jeweler cut each plate in half so that some diners were served two half-plates of melon while others were served two half-plates of a slow food dried Dutch ham, forcing guests to exchange dishes in order to enjoy a whole serving.

this page and opposite | For a meal choreographed for Droog Design, Vogelzang suspended the tablecloth from the ceiling, concealing signs of status like clothing, cut plates in half so that they had to be passed around to complete every meal, and asked guests to use unusual eating utensils. opposite above and right | For a physics conference and a 2008 gallery exhibition, Vogelzang's Photosynthesis Tree used the bulbs from Anglepoise task lamps to bake small biscuits.

IV. TECHNIQUE AND MATERIAL

There are an uncountable number of ingredients. | Likewise, there are so many techniques – bake, steam, grill, smoke, fry, pressurize, dehydrate, drill, sew, cut, print, knit, micro-cuisine, macro-cuisine, workshop-cuisine.

Vogelzang's work is about both concern and whimsy. It is one part psychology to one part sensuality, an interrogation of convention and an interrogation of oneself, science and social experiment. It is also one long and expressive investigation into materials: edible cutlery, salads made from ingredients grown in the dark. It is making meals (like Marcel Wanders' porcelain doodles) in 60 seconds, or baking root vegetables inside ceramic and asking guests to smash them open using hammers and mallets. Vogelzang's Photosynthesis Tree was originally designed for a physics conference. Hanging pendulously from a wooden 'tree', the bulbs illuminating a series of Anglepoise task lamps were used as a surface and a heat source that served in lieu of an oven or the sun. *'The tree produced food – leaf-shaped biscuits – by harnessing the energy and light from desk lamps,'* explains the designer. *'Their heat functioned as a 'stove' to bake the dough leaves, which were ready when they became crunchy and golden brown and fell to the ground like autumn leaves.'*

V. GROW

Origins, Seasons, and Cycles – Where do ingredients come from? Can you blame people that have survived a war for wanting strawberries in winter? What changes when we eat the seeds, the sprouts, the leaves, the flowers, the fruits of the same plant, what are the differences in taste? | **Education** – Teaching our children that milk doesn't grow on trees.

The Photosynthesis Tree was recreated for a summer 2008 exhibition entitled *'FUEL'* at Rotterdam's Showroom Mama. The show surveyed Proef's work with several installations and included a cuddly looking free-range pork and beef sausage. Reminding us to respect the fact that what we eat are creatures who must be butchered, Vogelzang made a sausage inside a tube of knitted wool that looked like a cartoon character: *'We eat meat,'* the artist's statement read, *'but the meat that we find in supermarkets doesn't look like a real animal. It's packaged in plastic. Everywhere around us we see cute animals on TV, in childrens' books, in commercials, etc. They look cute, have big eyes, wear clothes and sometimes they sing songs.'* The yarn swaddling the 200-kilo sausage, visitors were told, could be unraveled and, of course, eaten.

A second installation was viral: It began with just a few harmless marshmallows mounted to a wall and grew daily to cushion the entire space, walls, ceiling and floor, just as one begins with one bite of dessert and then eats the whole box, bag or pint. As the walls were taken over, the room filled with the saccharine scent of the sweets and its acoustics changed audibly. Vogelzang recalled for visitors the game Chubby Bunny in which children compete to see who can say *'Chubby bunny!'* with the most marshmallows stuffed into their cheeks, and then pointed out that in several cases, children (and even adults) have died playing this game. *'One marshmallow is cute and innocent,'* she writes, *'but when small things get big, you can get into trouble.'*

VI. PSYCHOLOGY

Memory Through Eating – Food does not only go down to your stomach but also up to your head. | **Seduction** – Why do we eat when we are not hungry? | **Social Rules.** | **Food as a Healer.** | **Rewarding with Food** – Children make mental connections between good behaviour and sweets. | **Food made with love gives the eater love through food.**

Sometimes Proef's work feels magical, at other times it can appear morbid. But in getting intimate with human beings, morbidity is sometimes unavoidable. Vogelzang has occasionally watched her guests moved to tears during her meals. For the Historical Museum of Rotterdam, she once reproduced original World War II rations in a meal prepared for veterans for whom the tastes brought back a flood of memories and a glut of emotions. Emotions, Vogelzang seems to suggest, are all good.

above from left | A free-range pork and beef sausage dressed in knitted wool for a gallery exhibition; the product designer's Hamman sculpture, made of ham.

FOOD ACTIVISTS : MARIJE VOGELZANG

VII. THE ACTION OF FOOD

Feeding someone is a very intimate action. | **Sharing food.** | **Surrounding and Environment** — Eating in a freezing cold room will be a very different sensation than eating in a comfortably temperate room. | **Body Position** — Are you lying down, sitting up, walking while you eat? | **Cutlery** — Is there any used? What happens to eating when using chopsticks or banana-leaves? | **Cooking Together.**

Memories recalled by eating were also cathartic in a 2008 community-building exercise called 'Taste of Beirut' that took place in the city's first farmers' market. Here, Vogelzang interviewed 100 locals, asking which foods they associated with their destructive and intractable (1978-1990) civil war. Bread, she heard, again and again, so Vogelzang used parsley juice to colour dough that a diverse group of residents formed into bowls on which they inscribed pleasant food memories before baking them. The bowls were then lined up at the farmers market to form a small-scale, metaphorical Green Line (the arbitrary line that separated the city's warring factions, the predominantly Muslim community in West Beirut from Christians in the east) before being offered to passers-by to eat with ricotta and local cedar honey. By sharing and consuming good memories, both bread and the Green Line were broken.

clockwise from left | Hardtack bread bowls dyed with parsley juice bore the stories of Beirut's civil war survivors; Vogelzang's laboratory and playground, Proef Amsterdam, opened in September 2006 with an interior designed by Onno Donkers in the Westergasfabriek park, an area populated with 'cultural entrepeneurs,' a daycare, graphic design offices, a theatre and a cinema

VIII. SOCIETY

Mass production | Sustainability | Energy use for production | Hygiene laws. | Politics. | Fishing in an empty sea. | World hunger and starvation. | Excess milk production. | Industrial food. | Chemical additives.

Vogelzang observes the environment around her, noticing ordinary things that most of us take for granted: processed foods found in supermarkets that don't look like real food and vegetarian alternatives to meat that shouldn't look like the real thing, but do. It was because she noticed that varying pH levels, water hardness, and mineral content make water taste different in different locations that Vogelzang disgorged water from the country's 12 provincial capitals into 130 liter-bottles each (equivalent to the amount consumed by one individual each day). With these bottles, she created a four-week installation during which visitors were encouraged to drink the water like various varietals of wine. In the end, she demonstrated that 'as with wine, terroir is very important' to the character of water.

While most chefs focus exclusively on the food, Vogelzang believes that food is already '*designed*' by nature. She wants to talk about social issues through nature's abundant materials palette and no conversation is too frivolous to have: the malnutrition created by starvation and the malnutrition that accompanies obesity, the lack of taste in old age or the lack of teeth, mass production versus provenance, the snuffing out of biodiversity, or the dilemma of '*food miles*'. For a city walk in Rotterdam, Vogelzang served food found only within city limits: dandelions, daisies and other weeds accompanied pigeon and locally produced honey. Her urban-eco dinner project comprised food that city residents could gather for free: long-neglected weeds, nuts, mushrooms, edible flowers and ducks, duck eggs and rats.

The project, explains Vogelzang, dealt with four of the eight points that she uses to map her work

'*1. Society*
_*We fly our food around the world. This is the most local way to harvest food.*
2. Psychology
_*Who dares to eat a rat?*
3. Culture
_*In other cultures it's very normal to eat weeds and pigeons and rats.*
4. Grow | History
_*Where does our normal food come from?*
_*It used to be normal to eat weeds. Weeds are a forgotten herb.*'

Addendum: A Note on Shit

The other (deliberately, blushingly) forgotten item, crucial to every meal? The title of Vogelzang's 2008 monograph, Posh Poo: Design That Goes Inside Your Body not only brings her work full circle, but keeps that circle going. Shitting is both the coda and the starting point of eating, as the product designer is well aware. '*I think shit is a very interesting point when it comes to eating design,*' she says. '*In an exhibition of mine in Rotterdam, visitors could weigh themselves before going to the toilet and then write down the difference after weighing themselves again afterwards.*' What we put in, must come out. Make it count.

FOOD ACTIVISTS : THE FOODISTS

Palettes for palates

The Berlin and Hamburg-based Foodists combine food, design, art and choreography to design artfully evocative events. *'What we do is about the total atmosphere, not only between the people, but also related to the room, or the purpose of the event,'* says Foodists creative director Telse Bus. *'The focus is to work from inside, trying to interpret an image or translate a feeling.'* Indeed, their meals may serve corporate clients ranging from Diesel, Lucky Strike and Adidas to Louis Vuitton but they are as expressive as a whisper – via taste, appearance and touch, in particular. The Foodists don't shape an event; they allow the event (its immediate intent, as well as the character of the company hosting it) to shape the meal and the environment in which it takes place.

Some dishes the Foodists create take on the most abstract of forms, so that guests can't trust their eyes; instead they must rely on the sense of taste. Or they will design a way to serve the food that is, as Bus phrases it, *'mummylike'*; rather than just tasting, they remember feelings elicited by the presentation as a whole. The Foodists' Classic Collection (a second collection is called *'Pop'* – both reminiscent of fashion lines) consists of

traditional dishes but with a modernised, and miniaturised, appearance. Creative Chef Martin Schanninge's *'Chicken on a Line'* is a well-composed still-life of a stuffed fowl, drumsticks akimbo in the air above the plate, cleaved perfectly in two to reveal the colour and texture of the herbed potato stuffing as if it were a polished geode. This nature morte is finished with a line of tomato drawn along the plate at the base of the bird like a streak of blood, as exquisitely grisly as any Old Master still-life. Unexpectedly, neither Foodist studied the culinary arts. Bus is a fine artist who, inspired by shamanism's use of flora and fauna (including edible items) as tools of emotional healing and communication, later began to work with food. Schanninger studied film before becoming a student of Berlin-based, Michelin-starred chef Kolja Kleeberg. He and Bus met while working together on the food concept for Copenhagen's Volkswagen FOX restaurant.

As their backgrounds suggest, The Foodists' intention is to engage all the senses in the service of expressing something essential about a brand, campaign or artwork. Cascette is The Foodist's atelier, where the work – in the form of free private dinners with carefully formulated guest lists – is imagined most lavishly. Guests sit close to the chef, mixing intimately with each other and with an artist whose canvases are displayed around them and echoed in the meal, itself. Schanninger translates the artwork into recipes and menus. To evoke one artist who used only muddy colours and textural flourishes in his paintings, Schanninger created visually appealing and tasty dishes without the use of red, yellow or light colours – or the flavours that accompany bright foods. On these evenings, in particular, it becomes clear that The Foodists don't merely cook up a palette for the palate; they create sensual environments that are as expressive as art.

---

top left | An amuse-bouche made from elder blubber with avocado and mixed berries.   below | A dish from The Foodists' POP catered food collection, marshmallows made from pistachio and blackberry.

this page | Scenes from The Foodists' private Berlin tasting room, Cascette, where art and food whose appearance, flavours and spirit reflects that of the art, come together with a select guest list

CASCETTE
A ROOM

KARL MARX ALLEE 75
10243 BERLIN

WWW.CASCETTE.DE
C@CASCETTE.DE

FOOD ACTIVISTS : ERICH STEKOVICS

Consider the Tomato

Austrian farmer and food visionary Erich Stekovics never tires of walking over his fields, tasting roots, seeds and shoots, squeezing the fruit just-so to measure its juice, sucking seeds out gently to taste them individually. Over and over again, he bends down, digs his hands into the soil to pull something out and pop it into his mouth with a thoughtful expression; his fingernails are perennially darkened with dirt. When Stekovics talks about his work, his entire ruddy face smiles and broadens. On his 33-hectare farm, amidst orchards, hives and rows of onions, gaggles of geese and knots of garlic, Stekovics cultivates 3,200 tomato varieties.

Consider the tomato. A much-maligned and oft-debated fruit (not vegetable). In days of yore, the Dutch tomato was the vilest villain of all: hardly touching the earth as it is grown, soaked in fertilizers, pesticides or other chemicals and arriving at the market both bruised and bland. Now it's the Spanish tomato that is the subject of calumny. In the U.S.

today, fingered as the source of regular outbreaks of salmonella, the poor tomato is the object of fruitless scrutiny since subject zero of the epidemic is usually never identified. The tomato has become the symbol of industrialised nature and, usually, a failure of both man and Mother Nature.

Stekovics, however, looks at the tomato anew, as both scientist and artist, historian and poet. Hundreds of years ago, there were more than 300,000 pure varieties of the tomato; at markets in Europe, shoppers find 10 types of hybrid tomato today. Stekovics is finding and carefully recovering thousands of previously lost types. The oldest that he has recovered is a 1,400-year-old Peruvian fruit, a tiny, sweet, tough-skinned yellow tomato. Others were lost in the 16th, 17th or 18th centuries. Most come from Stekovics' own region in Burgenland, but he also has a *very important collection* of Russian seeds from St. Petersburg. Why recover lost species of edible plants? *'Because particularly in these old varieties there is wonderful taste and aroma,'* Stekovics explains. *'The new sorts don't have it.'*

Stekovics has also returned craftsmanship to food production. His father worked a one-field farm, growing peppers and tomatoes, when Stekovics was a child and he established the Burgenland farm in 2002. *'I always wanted to work with all kinds of seeds of different vegetables and fruits,'* the farmer says, *'because I knew from my childhood the aroma of these wonderful old sorts.'* Today he grows garlic, sweet peppers and 560 varieties of chilli pepper, and cucumbers that are arranged in jars and slow-simmered compotes made from strawberries, apricots, marberries, raspberries and cherries and sold in Austria, Germany, Switzerland and Italy. Everything is harvested, cleaned, scraped, stirred and arranged in jars by hand.

Other farmers grow plants in greenhouses, but Stekovics always grows his produce *'out on the fields under the sun'* doing everything organically. *'We train the plants when they are very young,'* he says, *'before they are put out in the fields in May, so that they can survive outside.'* Stekovics even began to grow several hundred tomato varieties (in the shelter of a vast windshield) in the severe, sand-scoured deserts of Qatar at an invitation from the sheikh in 2006.

Stekovics, himself, walks the fields every day, checking on the plants, popping fruit into his mouth to test taste and aroma. Once upon a time he studied theology and the new career seems of a piece with this early calling. *"When he started there was just this one field, we had no machines. He started with nothing,"* says Stekovics' wife. *'He always remembered the taste from when he was a child. Always the taste.'*

above | Austrian organic farmer Erich Stekovics is still inspired by the tastes and smells of the plants his father grew when he was a child.

_ *'We train the plants when they are very young - before they are put out in the fields in May, so that they can survive outside.'*

| Today, on a 33-hectare farm, he grows 3200 species of tomato, many rescued from extinction through careful research; Stekovics spends a lot of time walking the fields, looking, smelling and tasting the crops.

STEKOVICS

capsicum
annuum
manibus
tractatum

FOOD ACTIVISTS : THE GHETTO GOURMET

Welcome to the table

With its skull and crossed fork and spoon, the Ghetto Gourmet is a homey scion of the speakeasy. In early 2004, leading a trend away from costly restaurants with wearisome gimmicks and poor service (and tables-for-two that lock diners into a single conversation all evening) and back to more social and adventurous eating, Jeremy Townsend started Ghetto Gourmet in his brother Joe's basement apartment in Oakland, California as a Monday night '*pirate restaurant*'. Joe used his one night off from cooking at a San Francisco restaurant and, by inviting friends, chatting up strangers on the street and strangers in supermarket check-out lines, putting out word-of-mouth online, and placing an ad on the ever-helpful Craigslist, the brothers would seat a dozen or so guests on floor cushions at low tables and offer a tasting menu accompanied by Miller High Life beer. At first, Townsend would show guests his tallied grocery store receipts, add 20% and split it among them. When Joe moved north, Jeremy continued to host Monday evenings in his East Bay Craftsman home, now seating up to 45 guests at a time at tables he'd made from old closet doors.

After a visit from a health inspector in early 2006, however, the unlicensed Ghetto Gourmet became a '*wandering supperclub*', and Townsend went on to produce over 350 dinners in galleries, homes and warehouses across the U.S., including L.A., Chicago, Miami, Tampa, Nashville and New York City. When the Townsends first began, Jeremy knew of only a few, as he calls them, '*online social dining projects*'; three years later, a New York Post article reviewed 15 in the New York metropolitan area alone.

Though commonplace in Eastern Europe, Cuba and Hong Kong, the move toward speakeasy eating is relatively new in the U.S., where restaurants are monitored and busted for the best of reasons. It seems most common, however, for guerrilla eateries like Townsend's to be run by those who tend to be conscientious: chefs looking for creative channels and serious foodies who are usually out to break even more than make a buck. Again and again, it is called a labour of love. In fact, it is usually gourmands in the know (often local chefs) who are first in attendance. And diners can get a $$$$ meal for $. For $30 (and a BYOB beverage of choice), a four or five-course meal might include anything from rabbit or duck confit to fried grasshoppers. And, as Townsend has been quoted as saying, as long as you keep your voice down, you can make out on the front porch.

| With its skull and crossed fork and spoon, and always a few steps ahead of health inspectors, the itinerant Ghetto Gourmet put on over 350 guerrilla eating events around the US before closing shop in 2008. For a fraction of the cost of an equivalent restaurant meal, foodies enjoyed adventurous meals that included making new friends around tables sometimes made from old doors.

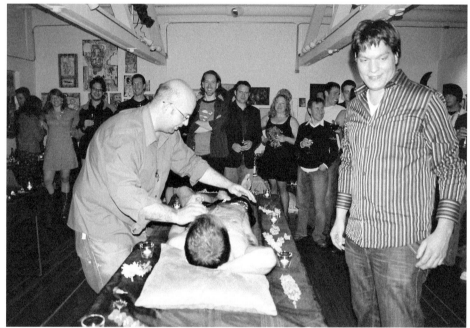

FOOD ACTIVISTS : ALEXANDRE BETTLER

Shared food and friendship

Starting with two 2.5m loaves of sourdough and rye bread and the French word for friend, '*copain*', or someone you break bread with ('*co*' meaning '*with*' and '*pain*' meaning '*bread*'), London-based designer Alexandre Bettler created The Bread Friend Map for the Gradual exhibition during the 2007 London Design Festival. Each visitor was offered a morsel from the long loaves. In return, they were asked to add stickers with their names on them to the wall and to connect their names via dotted lines to anyone else they knew on the map. This illustrated everyone's connection to other people and to those with whom they had shared the bread. The idea was to both demonstrate and generate connections: As the size of the loaf diminished, the larger the map became and the more friends there were.

Bettler's Bread Faces project, in collaboration with Marie Jean Lund, used sliced bread, jam, peanut butter and marmelade to allow people to paint portraits of friends and family on their snacks.

above and below | Bread Faces, Village Fete 2005. **right and opposite** | Gradual exhibition — The Bread Friend, 2007.

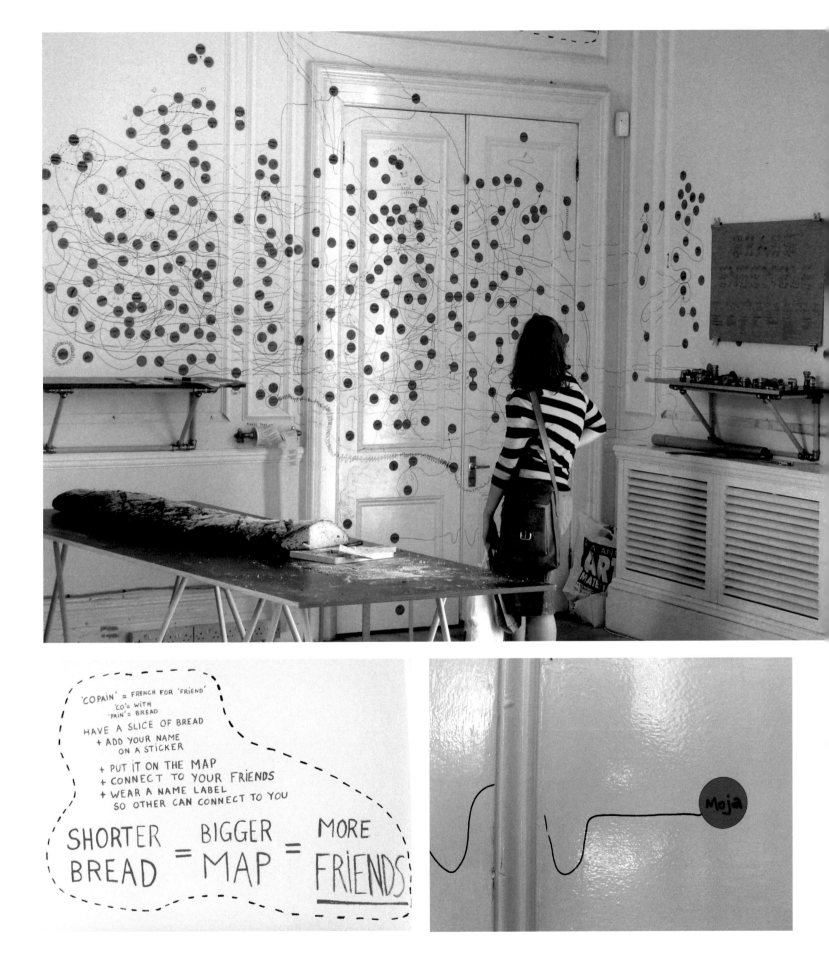

create.

'COPAIN' = FRENCH FOR 'FRIEND'
'CO'= WITH
'PAIN'= BREAD

HAVE A SLICE OF BREAD
+ ADD YOUR NAME
ON A STICKER

+ PUT IT ON THE MAP
+ CONNECT TO YOUR FRIENDS
+ WEAR A NAME LABEL
SO OTHER CAN CONNECT TO YOU

SHORTER BREAD = BIGGER MAP = MORE FRIENDS

moja

WHOLE HEAR/ TED.

'People increasingly want simplicity and traditionalism in food. There's less confidence in where food comes from, how it gets from A to B and the treatment of animals before slaughter. Those are the fashionable concerns. Simplicity in cooking is reassuring. Home-style cooking also allows people to eat out more often. People have less time to cook at home – that's becoming the special occasion.'

_ Tom Aikens, *chef and owner of Tom Aikens and Tom's Kitchen*

WHOLEHEARTED

Today we are watching the rise of a 21st century attitude to thrift that harks back to the canny approach of our grandmothers and places cheap yet high-quality produce at the heart of our diets. The new '*thrifter*' transcends the economic downturn by committing to more considered shopping, eating with integrity and proactively avoiding wastefulness.

This translates into being more aware of what represents good value: spending more for better quality ingredients and extracting every bit of their worth, shopping strategically and in tune with the seasons, or revisiting granny-approved, less expensive, less well-known cuts of meat. In terms of dining out, the '*gastro-thrifter*' is turning back to the honest comfort food served in canteen-style eateries, gastro-pubs and in the '*bistronomiques*' (casual eateries with less expensive menus that still feature high-level technical finesse) of Paris, Barcelona, New York and beyond.

These shifts, toward a more 'wholehearted' way of approaching food, mean that we are asking more questions, demanding more transparency, reassessing how to shop and eat, and, perhaps surprisingly, referring back to the reasoned advice of the relatives who lived through both WWII and the Depression. 'Most of what we need to know about how to eat we already know, or did until we allowed the nutrition experts and the advertisers to shake our confidence in the testimony of our senses and the wisdom of our mothers and grandmothers,' says Michael Pollan, author of In Defense of Food. 'Food should be about pleasure and family.'

Shifting ground

The backlash against the constantly shifting warnings (and, sometimes more ominously, the lack of warnings) of nutritional science, bolstered by a powerful, multimillion-dollar food marketing machine, is a particularly strong factor in the current move back to basics. Most controversially, the latest evidence seems to show that the fats our foremothers used are far better for our health than non-butter hydrogenated vegetable oil substitutes. Dr. Walter Willett of the Harvard School of Public Health in the US suggests that the transfats in butter substitutes that claim to be healthy could cause as many as 100,000 premature deaths, as they clog the arteries. Butter from grass-fed cows, however, is rich in the newly discovered K2 vitamin that helps build healthy bones and prevent calcification of arteries, while the much-maligned lard consists largely of unsaturated oleic acid, the same fat found in olive oil.

In December 2006, New York City became the first city to ban restaurants' use of artificial transfats. Eating establishments were given until July 2007 to make the switch to trans fat-free

opposite page | Natoora fruit and vegetable box sourced direct from individual farmers from Britain, France and Italy. **this page from left** | Crabapple jelly from Prince Charles' Highgrove organic grocery store. Products sold in the store are sourced from Home Farm on his estate.

frying oils and one year more – until July 2008 – to remove all transfats from their menus. Though controversial, like the smoking prohibition that preceded it, the ban passed the city's Board of Health by a unanimous vote.

Nina Planck, the author of Real Food: What to Eat and Why and a pioneer of the modern farmers' market, says, 'In our house we eat traditional foods with impunity. So go ahead and eat your butter: it's good for you.'

Exposés and celebrity appeals

Books such as Not on the Label: What Really Goes into the Food on Your Table, by leading investigative food journalist Felicity Lawrence, and exposés such as Shopped by Joanna Blythman, have fuelled greater awareness. These critiques reveal both the health and environmental consequences of over-processed food, ready meals and the buy-one-get-one-free supermarket offers that contribute to so much waste. Recent graphic media coverage of battery chicken farms has made consumers increasingly aware of the impact of their bargain shopping bill and has raised ethical concerns over what exactly they are buying. When celebrity chefs Jamie Oliver, Gordon Ramsay and Hugh Fearnley-Whittingstall combined to highlight the false economy of cheap chicken, the message was also brought home to a wider number of shoppers. Supermarkets are suddenly finding that the booming demand for free-range chicken – up 35% during January 2008 on the same period the previous year – is exceeding current supply.

Learning how to eat

A new campaign addressing Britain's wasteful attitude towards food was launched in October 2007 and advocates leftovers as a cheaper, greener option to buying more. The Waste and Resources Action Programme (WRAP) claims that a third of all food bought in the country's high streets ends up in the bin, which adds up to 6.7m tonnes of discarded food, or £8bn, per year.

According to WRAP chief executive Dr Liz Goodwin, 90% of consumers are unaware of the amount of food they throw away. 'Once attention is drawn to it, however, we know that people are surprised and keen to take action,' says Goodwin. The WRAP campaign features a website with advice on preparation, storage and portioning, along with recipes that can help to cut down food and packaging waste. Meanwhile, food magazine Delicious recently introduced 'Loose Ends', a section devoted to using up leftovers creatively, an addition that is proving to be wildly popular with readers.

Putting an end to waste

Today, it is trailblazing chefs and restaurateurs who are in the vanguard when it comes to raising awareness of wastefulness and other green and sustainability issues alongside food provenance and frugality.

'Restaurants have to wake up to being such a wasteful business, especially as the bottom line will increasingly matter in the success of a restaurant,' says Jamie Grainger-Smith, general manager of Acorn House restaurant in London. *'It's equally important to restaurant-goers, to the extent that they might pick one restaurant over another. It's important to provide an experience to consumers without ramming values down their throats, but more and more consumers are seeking out environmental info on where they eat, as on other consumer goods they buy. Even the way menus are written will reflect this: providing more options on portion sizes, for instance, to minimise waste.'*

Consumers' growing awareness of the amount of waste produced by over-packaged food and supermarket goods was boosted by the astounding popularity of Anya Hindmarch's *'I'm Not A Plastic Bag'*. Produced in collaboration with the global social change movement and launched in Anya Hindmarch stores, the limited-edition canvas tote bag was also sold in conjunction with Sainsbury's and Whole Foods markets. Each person in the UK uses an average of 167 plastic carrier bags every year, a total of 10bn bags. In January 2008, in a bid for good press preceding the Beijing summer Olympics, China joined several others countries (including Ireland and even Uganda) in banning free plastic bags from its supermarkets and small shops, a move it admits will save 37m barrels of crude oil each year. In Taiwan, the whole country is getting in on the act:

not only have plastic bags been banned, but also the disposable plastic plates, cups and cutlery used by street vendors. Fines of up to £152 have already reduced usage of plastic bags by 70%, producing a 25% drop in landfill waste. Meanwhile, Ireland's 15p tax on plastic bags has resulted in a 90% reduction in their use since 2002. In 2007, San Francisco, where 180m plastic bags were distributed every year, became the first US city to ban plastic bags. Supermarkets and large pharmacies are only able to offer corn-starch or recycled paper bags. Today, we are seeing the rise of *'unpackaging'*: well-designed products designed to be refilled and a far cry from the dingy Tupperware that many consumers associate with re-usable food containers.

The death of cheap

Nielsen's research in 47 markets worldwide confirms the rise of gastro-thrift. Nielsen found that an overwhelming 85% of consumers cited *'good value for money'* as the most important consideration when choosing a grocery store. Recently, shoppers have been polarised by two seemingly opposing trends that both point to the rise of thrift. TNS Worldpanel grocery market figures for January 2008 show low-end supermarkets Morrisons, Aldi and Lidl are experiencing a great deal of success because they are known for giving good value for the money. At the other extreme, premium supermarket Waitrose's is growing more popular too, as shoppers decide that they are willing to pay more in order to get greater value on the dollar.

And this is a good thing, because: *'Cheap food is not cheap,'* says In Defense of Food author Michael Pollan. *'You end up paying eventually, either in the environmental cost, or as a society you pay in public health costs.'* Restaurateur Fergus Henderson, author of The Whole Beast: Nose-to-Tail Eating, agrees. *'Good meat is not meant to be niche; good butchers should not be a boutique operation. People should spend lots on food and use it all. Now you have people spending £1.99 on a chicken and they get used to pink flobby meat in plastic, having forgotten what quality meat is.'*

Most food has seemingly become cheaper and cheaper over the last decade, as supermarkets compete fiercely on price, and *'basics'* ranges supply cheap food to the less well-off, even if its quality is questionable. However, prices that have been kept consistently below inflation look set to soar as rising oil prices, grain scarcity, unpredictable climates and growing demand in emerging economies push up prices in the West. Food inflation could be a serious concern in the near future, as prices are driven up by scarcity of cereal crops that feed livestock, as well as being used for basic human foodstuffs. In the US, wheat stocks are at their lowest since 1947, while corn stores are down

left | The Olde Bell Inn, Hurley, one of a series of traditional coaching inns redesigned by StudioIlse.

Grandmother's cooking

Definition | A universally understood, affectionate term which is tinged with nostalgia; it describes old-fashioned, heart-warming, familiar dishes, usually hearty and comforting, as well as frugal and thrifty.

A simple frosted cake rather than macaroons and fancy cupcakes

Slow-braised beef rather than sirloin

A Dutch-oven stew rather than pan-fried monkfish

Home-baked chocolate chip cookies rather than the ubiquitous lemon tart and chocolate fondant

Frittata and fresh fruits rather than hummus, wraps and crisps on picnics

Marshmallows toasted on the bonfire

by 20%. '*Pricing is the biggest concern among consumers, especially as the industry strives towards higher quality all the time,*' says David Swinghamer, Co-owner of the Union Square Hospitality Group, New York. '*How much is the customer prepared to pay for any one item? It's the fundamental foods such as bread and dairy that are seeing the real increases.*'

Indeed, how will a generation of shoppers used to buying premium, organic and artisanal goods respond to the rising cost of staples such as bread, butter, milk and eggs? According to recent reports, we could be on the cusp of the kind of global food shortage not seen since the 1970s. According to IGD, the food retail industry's education body, most UK shoppers under 50 will never have experienced inflation related to food prices. However, in 2007, the overall inflation rate in the UK was 2.1%, while the food-price inflation rate was 5.9%. According to the Office for National Statistics, prices rose by 12% in the UK during 2007, a £750 hike in the average family's food bill. As a result, we're seeing the return of label-watching, with even more affluent shoppers determined to get the best value for money.

In Mexico, West Bengal, Morocco, Senegal and Yemen, we have already seen food riots over the escalating prices of staple foods such as maize and corn. While we are unlikely to experience the same in the West, we will see a growing unease about rocketing prices for basic goods. Critics are placing much of the blame on the recent boom in ethanol fuel production, which requires tracts of land to be turned over to monocultured crops such as corn, sugar cane and rapeseed. According to The Economist, the 30m tonnes of corn being turned over to ethanol production account for half the fall in global grain stocks. Some environmentalists claim that growing grain and processing it into ethanol uses more energy from fossil fuels than ethanol actually generates.

The revival of value

Nowadays, food-savvy and value-minded consumers are returning to shopping in traditional butchers. There is a revival of older, native breeds: Belted Galloway and Longhorn beef cattle, Gloucester Old Spot and Tamworth pigs, Herdwick and Dorset Horn sheep. Well-hung meat, such as 28-day steak from a named heritage breed, is a prestige dish in the top gastro-pubs. Besides better service and advice, butchers offer a fuller range of cuts and '*nose to tail*' alternatives. These range from pork belly to shin of beef, oxtail, bone marrow and lambs' tongues and are ultra-modish worldwide, featuring particularly in Michelin-starred chefs' '*bistronomiques*'.

above | Chickens prepared by Rosie Sykes, chef at The Olde Bell Inn.

CASE STUDY | Canteen

Canteen, currently in Spitalfields and on the South Bank, London, is one of the great successes of granny-style, democratic, gastro-thrift food. Canteen's all-day menu offers reasonably priced, *'honest'* food of sound and seasonal provenance.

The concept has won countless awards, including the Which? Good Food Guide London Restaurant of the Year. The two restaurants currently serve 5,000 – 7,000 covers each week and a new West End branch will open this summer.

The menu includes dishes such as potted duck with piccalilli and toast, which feature in the larder lexicon of grandmothers' cooking, alongside devilled kidneys on toast, thrifty cuts of meat and pies served with mash, greens and proper gravy. Canteen's range of puddings and cakes is also granny-inspired: treacle tart, shortbread fingers, Victoria sponge and ginger cake.

Chris Galvin, owner of Galvin Bistrot de Luxe, believes that instead of buying cuts such as fillet and sirloin, restaurants should buy shoulder and neck, '*even when using venison*'. These take longer to cook but offer more intense flavour, explains Galvin. '*Braising the cheaper cuts results in some fantastic dishes. [Restaurants should] buy ingredients only at the height of their season when they are at their cheapest, too*'.

Slow and sure

Everywhere, there is a renewed elegance and quality seen in meats over which we must take our time. '*The trend for these slow-cook cuts is happening all over Europe,*' says Stefan Kolsch, head chef at Donald Russell, an online butcher that sells premium-quality, grass-fed, naturally reared and fully matured meats. '*It started in the US with the* "slow food" *movement, which was really a response to the hated fast-food culture that is sweeping the world today.*'

Such cuts are popular for their depth of flavour, intrinisic value and capacity, in our busy times, for being prepared ahead of time without losing quality. They also symbolise a return to a more traditional way of cooking. '*It takes time and effort to cook them, but it's such a wonderful experience to turn a humble, inexpensive cut into something delicious, with an intensity of flavour that you just don't get from a normal roast or steak,*' insists Kolsch. '*Our most popular slow-cook cut is without doubt our richly marbled beef rib trim, followed by shin of beef. It's a return to simplicity and traditional cooking methods – the way our grandmothers used to feed their families.*'

Cooking with these more economical cuts requires more time and no little expertise; not always practical for harried professionals, which goes some way to explaining why comfort dishes are so popular when dining out. As Michael Pollan suggests, '*Cooking has historically been the way people without a lot of money get a lot of value from a small amount of food: stews, soups, creative ways with leftovers and organs. If you don't have the money, you do have to put in the time. If you say you don't have the money or the time, you're going to be stuck eating junk food, which isn't even as cheap as it looks.*'

Allegra McEvedy, co-founder of "*fresh fast food chain*" – imagine if you will: carefully sourced seasonal ingredients, low prices, low-carb and low-GI, vegetarian and allergy-friendly, gluten-free, dairy-free and sugar-free, free-range and fair trade, all delivered with the speed of fast food! – Leon, also believes that slow cooking is the way forward, '*using cheap, full-of-flavour cuts such as shanks, neck, belly or shoulder, which we've been*

throwing in the bin, which is nothing short of a crime. It's all about getting organised to free up your time, as these dishes take care of themselves.'

As a result, time-poor gastro-thrifters are fuelling a resurgence in sales of slow cookers and crock-pots, according to John Lewis, which are up 25% year-on-year. The department store notes that slow cookers, designed for moist-heat cooking, are being bought by busy professionals who are lured by the convenience of having a slow-braised meal ready when they get home from work. As an extra enticement, slow cookers are programmable, can keep food warm, are dishwasher safe, and perhaps best of all, are notably energy efficient, using less electricity than it takes to power a light bulb.

Eating a larger picture

As shoppers rediscover more frugal cuts of meat, they are also embracing other parts of the animal, fuelling a resurgence in whole-animal eating. Sales of beef and lamb offal have risen steadily year-on-year over the past three years, a trend that looks set to continue, with the lion's share of growth, nearly a third, at butchers' shops. Many buyers of offal (including '*specialities*' such as sweetbreads, fries, tripe and ox cheek) are influenced by its popularity among chefs today. '*So many people these days don't realise that offal is not only extremely delicious, but can be a total bargain,*' says respected food writer and broadcaster Sophie Grigson. '*In fact, I'd go as far as to say that it is one of the great neglected delicacies.*'

'*Whole-beast*' products are also becoming more widely available, raising their acceptability further. Fergus Henderson of the St. John restaurant has launched his first retail product, Trotter Gear or '*unctuous potential*', as he calls his lip-smacking, glutinous stock, enriched with pigs' trotters. This has long been a staple of his restaurant kitchen and comes into its own during slow cooking. Meanwhile, chef Tom Aikens recently launched a select range of ready meals from his Tom's Kitchen menu, exclusively for Selfridges. These include fresh stocks, alongside updates on thrifty dishes such as his signature braised lamb shoulder with balsamic onions.

Pre-eminent London butcher Allens of Mayfair has been overwhelmed by the demand for its new butchery classes, which teach skills from jointing a chicken to maximise its usage to preparing oxtail. Hugh Fearnley-Whittingstall's River Cottage butchery courses, which include working with a whole carcass or smoking and curing invariably sell out, even though most of his students are unlikely ever to rear their own pig. Leiths Cookery School reports that in 2008, carving skills classes were among the first to fill up, alongside preserving classes – another example of a renewed interest in thrifty cooking.

---

opposite page | Canteen, Spitalfields, London; fish dish served at Canteen.

Fishing for change

There's evidence of a parallel revival of the traditional fishmonger. Aside from a revived interest in carp, the eco-thrift consumer is increasingly aware of marine conservation issues and seeks out fishmongers with the passion and knowledge to sell local, line-caught, lesser-known or hitherto neglected species such as gurnard, megrim sole, Cornish anchovies and mackerel. Fish cheeks, long considered a delicacy in Basque Spain, put in increasing cameo appearances on chic menus in London and Paris. Less established, but likely to gain favor in restaurants, is the fish equivalent of nose-to-tail eating, celebrating parts that have often been discarded in the past.

At Madrid Fusion 2008, the world's most influential gastronomic conference, leading second-generation Spanish new wave chef Marcos Morán from the Casa Gerardo restaurant in Asturias eloquently advocated '*cooking with fish trash*'. This included tuna heart (long-considered a delicacy in that tuna-canning region) and red mullet liver.

In Newfoundland, cod's tongue has long been considered a delicacy. Usually fried in a light batter and topped with aioli or traditional '*scrunchions*', crispy snippets of salted pork, its gourmet allure lies in its gelatinous texture. Elsewhere, other glamorous A-list eateries are cooking at the forefront of the marine leftovers trend as well, celebrating cod's tongue and herring milt (roe) on toast, or monkfish cheeks with sauce gribiche.

senior retail analyst at Mintel believes that food miles are now high on the consumer agenda. '*People are becoming increasingly aware of just how far their food has had to travel.*' In Melbourne, the 100 Mile Café sources ingredients from a radius of no more than 100 miles. Each dish is labelled with the food mileage of its ingredients, so super-strict Localvores can choose their lunch on food miles alone. For example, pan-fried quail and herb potato galette with red wine teriyaki glaze and roast beetroot, blood orange salad, and cherry dressing has travelled an average of 76.25 miles, while tempura of Western Port garfish fillets with zucchini flowers stuffed with goat's cheese mousse clocks in at 52.6 miles. The Urban Rustic grocery and café in Williamsburg, Brooklyn, similarly prides itself on sourcing all its ingredients from local suppliers, harvested no more than 48 hours before they are served.

The Konstam restaurant in north London takes the idea further, sourcing all produce from within the M25 motorway, which circles the city. Masterminded by owner-chef Oliver Rowe, Konstam opened in April 2006. The restaurant was featured in a TV series that followed Rowe as he searched for locally sourced, seasonal food from all over the Greater London region. Today over 85% of the produce used in the Konstam kitchen is grown or reared from the area covered by the Underground network, and the menu features dishes named after source locations, such as Sevenoaks beef and Hillingdon salsa. Despite the growth in Localvore eateries, however, many consumers still feel they are not getting enough information about food miles from major retailers.

left | Tom's Kitchen products launched this year by chef Tom Aikens sold exclusively at selfridges.   above | All ingredients used in Moro East are sourced from Manor garden allotments, East London, designed by Here Design. **opposite page** | Interiors from the Matbaren restaurant in Stockholm designed by Ilse Crawford of StudioIlse, in her classic, eclectic style, marrying modern and traditional, austere and ornamental to create a fresh environment for a chef who is reinventing regional Swedish cuisine.

Gastro-thrifts to watch

Ad Hoc is a no-choice, casual, home-style dining restaurant run by Thomas Keller, who has three Michelin stars. The restaurant, in Yountville, California, majors on comfort food such as hearty soups, stews and ribs.

Meyers Deli in Copenhagen offers family-style dishes. Owner Claus Meyer is a leading TV personality and cookbook writer who campaigns for the New Nordic food movement and better food education.

Matbaren in Stockholm, with quirkily elegant interiors designed by Ilse Crawford, is the informal dining operation of Mathias Dahlgren, one of the chefs at the forefront of New Nordic cuisine. Matbaren's menu features modern interpretations of grandma's cooking, from herring, potato and dill salad to meatballs and apple and rye crumb dessert.

Bistronomiques such as Le Timbre, Café Burq and Le Bistrot Paul Bert in Paris are bringing cuisine grandmère and low prices to a new generation of cheap-chic Parisians.

Erdapfel in Frankfurt is a cool and minimalist German take on the gastro-pub, with an emphasis on dishes accompanied by potato since '*erdapfel*' is the Old High German word for that stridently starchy foodstuff.

THE REVOLUTION WILL BE ETHICAL

Changing ethical tastes, the return of thrift and a new generation of synthetic-friendly consumers are just a few of the many sparks that will ignite a revolution in how we create, market and consume food.

Flavour of the fields

Health and ethical concerns are creating a renaissance in game meats, many of which are low in fat and cholesterol. Sales are rocketing, fuelled by health-conscious female shoppers. Sales of grouse, venison and pheasant rose by 46% to £57m between 2004 and 2006 and are forecast to increase a further 47% to £84m by 2011. The market for game is now growing faster than that of traditional red meats, poultry and fish, with more supermarkets introducing game to their stores. As game meats are naturally free-range, they also appeal to consumers put off by intensive farming techniques. *'Today's growing concern about the environment and the negative impact of mass-produced food is changing the types of food we buy, with many of us opting for food that is organic, locally sourced, or bought from a farmers' market,'* says David Bird, senior market analyst at Mintel. *'As game comes from free-ranging animals and is wild and natural, this market is clearly perfectly placed to take full advantage of this trend.'*

On top of their game

Mintel predicts that the growing interest in game will push more foodies outdoors to catch their own food. Expect to find more people shooting and fishing as concerns over where their food comes from take them out into the fields.

Excessively packaged and processed foods are less appealing and consumers are responding by opting for the live, wild and home-reared. For a growing group of urban hunters, the premium lies in their participation in the food chain. The weekly food shop or evening of culinary experimentation is no longer sufficient. They seek a new type of eating experience, which taps into their hunter-gatherer roots. Hunting is booming as the urban hunter embraces rural traditions and turns to game as a lean alternative to beef, chicken or pork. A Mintel report reveals that venison, rabbit and pheasant have surged in popularity in recent years, with sales increasing by 46% to £57m between 2004 and 2006.

'The price of pheasant is tumbling down,' says Lady Onslow, who hosts pheasant shoots on her farmland in Clandon Park, Surrey. *'It's so popular now, so there are a great deal more shoots taking place and an excess of pheasants being reared for them.'* The shooting industry is booming, fuelled by corporate events and city boys who want to taste the action. *'It's very much about taking your pheasant home and eating it. The whole point about shooting is that whatever is shot, is eaten,'* says Lady Onslow.

Elsewhere, intrepid hunters are heading for the nearest woodland and filling their backpacks with nature's produce. For those who want guidance in the art of foraging, gourmet wilderness courses are growing in number. *'A lot of our courses are run for corporate teams who use the wilderness survival situation as a metaphor for team building in the office,'* explains Andrew Price, founder and head instructor of Dryad Bushcraft.

left | Pieminister award-winning hand made pies; Tom's kitchen products launched this year by chef Tom Aikens sold exclusively at Selfridges.

'*We are also popular with inner city youngsters, who learn that the outdoors is not a hostile place.*' Price teaches participants how to catch, prepare and cook meat, using traps and hunting tools, and how to identify out edible plants and berries. They learn how to catch and prepare rabbit, woodcock and squirrel, which is apparently great in a curry and tastes like chicken.

Celebrity chefs Jamie Oliver and Hugh Fearnley-Whittingstall have helped to open up this lifestyle to new audiences, and Price sees it in the context of a need to reconnect with the food on the table. '*There's a widespread desire to regain control over what we eat and where it comes from and foraging is just one part of this trend,*' he says. Elsewhere, consumers are taking the matter into their own hands and into their own backyards too. The urban micro-farm, complete with chickens and maybe a pig, is making a comeback. New York magazine journalist Manny Howard chronicled his attempt at urban farming and received rave reviews, and rumour has it there is a feature film on the way. Even restaurants are tapping in on the trend. Studio Müller en Van Tol's most recent project, Restaurant As in Amsterdam, features a window that overlooks the livestock bred for consumption in the restaurant. Could live wet markets, as seen in Asia, be next?

Organic growth

After gaining great ground, it seems that the organic food market may have reached saturation, with 2007's environmental problems blamed for the shortage in supply. Meanwhile, consumers are growing increasingly confused over what is better for them and the environment: organic, but possibly flown from Africa or Asia, or local, limiting food miles, but possibly containing pesticides.

The more information that people have access to, the more concerned they become about food issues such as organics, genetic modification, fat content and provenance. Imported organic produce now accounts for only 30% of the UK market, but organic box deliveries, now a staple in many middle-class households, are booming, thanks to the fact that their organic produce is local, offering the perfect combination for the well-informed foodie. Sales of organic boxes have more than doubled over the last two years (109%) to £150m.

Raw Rising

Another but more unexpected version of wholehearted eating? Raw. A raw food diet no longer carries connotations of long-haired hippies eating flowers in San Francisco. This trend, which developed among a group of serious health food enthusiasts in the US, has expanded globally, and is becoming relevant among consumers keen to adopt a more holistic approach to food. While the trend has been mainstream in the US for some time – with many raw food pioneers, such as David Wolfe – other countries have been slower to catch on. The raw food movement resonates with a generation that is time-poor, pollution-sensitive and health-conscious. It is about more than eating salad; it is an approach that champions purity and dietary control. Preparing raw food is often very complex, but the underlying concept is simple, and strikes a chord with those searching for balance in today's digital age of uncertainty.

Besides coming into its own in restaurants and cafes, raw food is slowly developing a presence in food shops too. The LÄRA-BAR, an energy bar made from pure whole ingredients, has appeared in several organic stores and in Selfridges, while Kensington's Whole Foods Market now has a section devoted to raw food products. And Waitrose is hot on their heels: Andrew

below | '*my sweets*' by Tithi Kutchamuch addresses issues such as overeating, eating disorders, obesity, illness, guilt and food waste. Kutchamuch subverts the idea of the supersized chocolate bar.

Davis, co-founder of The Raw Food School in London and a raw food chef, plans to release a raw food range with the supermarket. Even Pepsi is getting in on the uncooked act with Pepsi Raw, its new cola made from naturally sourced ingredients.

Microsizing

A wholehearted approach to eating includes an appreciation not just of monetary value but of the value of quality over quantity. The backlash against supersize portions is giving rise to microsizing. Smaller portions are increasingly appealing to waist-conscious and waste conscious consumers. In the US, where supersized portions are endemic, the industry has warned of consumer resistance to smaller portions because of perceived poor value. However, according to research by Harris Interactive, 47% of Americans have vowed to eat smaller portions in 2008.

Restaurants are beginning to take the controversial decision to offer smaller portions. For example, the TGI Friday chain's '*Right Portion, Right Price*' menu is beginning to pay off. '*Right Portion*' dishes are a third smaller than regular dishes and around 30% cheaper. Though the casual dining industry is facing a downturn, TGI's customer counts are on the up: the number of TGI customers has risen by 1.4%, while industry-wide customer counts have fallen by 2.8%.

The trend has also given rise to the growth of smallplate dining, which allows diners to choose from a wide menu of smaller dishes, giving greater control over portion size. Key examples include Minibar in Los Angeles, which offers a 39-item menu of international bites. Minnies in Chicago takes the idea even further, with a menu of bite-size gourmet burgers and sandwiches described as '*nouvelle cuisine portions for casual dining*'. Besides serving waistline-minded eaters something to nibble on, the 50s-style diner gives hungrier customers the mix-and-match pleasure of tapas restaurants.

The perception of value is the major hurdle in reducing portion sizes, and making less look like more will ultimately fall to packaging designers. RCA graduate Tithi Kutchamuch's most recent project addresses issues such as obesity, illness, guilt, food waste and over-production by subverting the idea of the supersized chocolate bar which may be a better value in dollars and cents but which is of poor value to one's health. While her packaging design is the same size as any supersized bar, the amount of chocolate inside is 20-30% less, with cut-out stenciling of the wrapper further decreasing the amount of candy in the packet.

Ready-prepared, set, go

Happily for those of us who are constantly on the go, wholehearted gastro-thrifters will fuel an increasingly discerning 21st-century market both for home cooking and eating out or take-away. The demand for fresh (and freezable) comfort-food dishes and meals based on historic recipes is huge, because of the time it takes to cook these from scratch. Forward-looking butchers and delis are starting to produce their own ready-prepared versions of these dishes. It's likely that an increasing number of chefs will be willing to put their name to such in-demand dishes, which will only increase their credibility and appeal to the well-informed shopper.

The American concept of cookshops, where cooking for the freezer becomes a social activity, may take off in Europe. Often the laborious aspects of the preparation, such as making stock or chopping vegetables, are already accomplished when the customer arrives, and is reflected in the price. Such cookshops also offer fresh or frozen meals such as fish pie or lasagne for those too busy to attend.

left | Pepsi Raw is made from natural ingredients and contains no artificial preservatives, colours, flavourings or sweeteners. Pepsi claims that by replacing corn syrup with cane sugar it has managed to reduce the calorie content of a 300ml bottle from around 120 calories to around 90 calories.

Supermarkets are already initiating a shift in the purchasing of frozen food to ensure seasonality and freshness. The benefits of frozen ingredients are becoming more widely known. For example, it's possible to eat seasonal fruit all year round, supporting local farms, as well as one's health, since freezing locks in nutrients. People are using their freezer as an extended store-cupboard and as a convenient facilitator for scratch cooking. People are buying more and more frozen fruit to get mixtures, as well as out-of-season varieties. Frozen vegetables like peeled and cubed butternut squash or prepared artichoke hearts, which cut cooking time but still offer versatility, are also experiencing greater popularity in the check-out line. And the trend shows no signs of abating.

Grown in transit

In stocking inventory, supermarkets and modern food transportation systems have sacrificed freshness and seasonality in favour of warehousing depots, bulk transportation and blemish-free produce. But a new attitude is emerging, with the creation of innovative ways of growing food in transit rather than refrigerating products into suspended animation.

Design Academy Eindhoven graduate Agata Jaworska's project *'Made in Transit'* aims to eliminate the wasted time and trapped inventory in many supply chains by actually growing produce en route to the store. Jaworska's concept aims to move from *'best before'* preservative packaging to *'ready by'* cultivational packaging which consumers would open when the product was ready for consumption.

below | Made in Transit by Agata Jaworska, a new system of mushroom cultivation shifting the role of distribution from slowing down the process of post-harvest deterioration to enabling growth and involving the consumer at the point of harvest.

Jaworska's first example would grow mushrooms on the way to the supermarket. *'The instant a crop is removed from the ground or separated from its parent plant, a steady process of deterioration begins,'* says Jaworska. *'Methods to compensate for the loss of quality, taste and nutrients can only slow the process of deterioration down, but the result will never match what we have at the source of life.'* The grown-in-transit concept enables growth along the way, to deliver absolute freshness and allow the consumer to *'harvest'* their own food. The idea would also minimise excess packaging, such as the plastic film and crates that protect delicate food items in transit. These are rarely re-used.

Award-winning chef Arthur Potts Dawson hopes to bring a community aspect to the trend with his *'veg barge'* concept. He plans to create an aquatic allotment on a barge, which would service restaurants by travelling up and down the canal as the herbs, fruits and vegetables grow. Potts Dawson is also keen to use the barge to serve the community, by promoting and selling locally grown foods.

The new heart of the home

Part of the wholehearted approach involves seeing not just one's food but also one's equipment as part of the solution. Designers who have noticed a lack of kitchen design development over the past three decades have begun to turn their attention to the hearth of the home and its appliances. Young designer Alex Bradley, for example, highlights the need to address social and cultural issues when designing for the kitchen space. He takes into account the rise in singleperson households, the resulting reduced living space sizes and the development of connectivity. Bradley's Single Person Cooker (SPC), with its wifi connection, modular design and adjoining website, responds to evolving eating habits and the pace and structure of daily life. Information made available via the integrated wifi screen helps the user create nutritious, healthy meals quickly and efficiently. The SPC aims to steer consumers away from ready meals, and create an object of focus and discussion in the kitchen. It was designed with the single person or commuter in mind: consumer groups whose time is precious and who are likely to find food preparation a chore. Bradley hopes to develop this lifestyle concept to enable the SPC appliance to integrate with SPC furniture, providing dual living and eating areas.

The one-pallet kitchen develops ideas of modularity and flexibility in what is traditionally a static space. It is a stackable kitchen made from wood chip and natural resin. The durable units are easy to assemble and require no glue or screws.

'Our design process is driven by function, where the function becomes the construction. One-pallet kitchen's stackable nature is a flexible kitchen for the flexible lifestyle of the future,' explain designers Steie van Vugt and Frank Winnubst of Frank&Steie.

Similarly, Feuer & Pfanne (Fire & Pan) is a mobile kitchen with integrated heat source, fuel supply, pans and food containers. Feuer & Pfanne was designed for the Dining in 2015 competition by Klein Oliver and Seebach Marie, in response to a brief set by macef milano and Designboom in 2008. It is neatly contained in a hinged box so the kitchen can easily be mounted and taken apart for cleaning. 'In a world of increasing mobility, we need solutions for every necessity, allowing us to be flexible and individual – even when it comes to food,' explain Oliver and Marie.

The Veneta Cucine concept by Dante Donegani and Giovanni Lauda is based around simple cooking techniques and encourages the user to explore new ways of using the kitchen. The space is divided up by simple pergola-like constructions with areas for wine, water, cooking, kitchen plants, utensils and even the family pet.

Old-fashioned cooking equipment with a modern design makeover is also seeing a renewal. Cuisinart has already updated the pressure cooker, with a brushed stainless steel version

---

above | Bradley's Single Person Cooker (SPC) by Alex Bradley.
opposite | Module Kitchen by Drift design. The different modules can be placed in different ways, against a wall or free in a space, even outside.

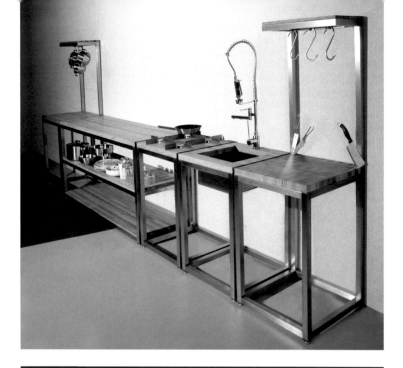

that cooks up to 70% faster than conventional pots, ideal for overwhelmed cook-it-yourselfers who want cosy, cost-saving comfort food when they return home at the end of a long workday. In the US, there is even a book by Beth Hensperger and Julie Kaufman devoted to slow cookers, the title of which says it all: Not Your Mother's Slow Cooker Cookbook.

From soup to nuts

Rather than sending people running for gourmet trappings and junkfood, the current economic downturn is pushing them to reassess the value of the food they buy and making their shopping trolley work harder. Shoppers are still rightly insisting on the same high-quality produce they discovered in the farmers' market boom, but with a renewed focus on getting the best and the most for their money. Buying steak hung for 28 days from a traceable farm is no longer enough, as consumers are choosing equally high-quality but old-fashioned cuts, such as beef skirt or brisket, that can be stretched further with a bit of care.

Value, then, has become the dealmaker when it comes to choosing from the grocer's shelves. Most people, when asked, say that companies and producers that offer value for money are likely to hold sway over their purchasing power in the coming year, while almost everyone insists that value is the most important benefit that their favourite brands provide.

But it's not just about money. This *"wholehearted"* approach to food is also a well-considered moral choice. People now tend to take a puritanical view of the massive (and inexcusable) inefficiencies of the modern food industry, from buy-one-get-one-free offers that leave them with products that are never used, to retailers' dismissal of less well-known cuts of meat and all but the highest-yield, highest-margin fruit and vegetables. However, for a generation raised on ready meals and microwaves, the growth of a wholehearted approach to cooking requires re-education. This means that food producers and retailers can do the public the service of making themselves experts on their products and authorities in their markets. Helping people to understand the value of what they buy and the environmental and ethical impact of their purchases is as valuable to us today as the product.

Food shops, markets and even restaurants can become not just places to shell out cash, but places to learn. This goes beyond the recipe cards that many supermarkets offer to promote their products, towards teaching people how to get the most out of their purchases with expert staff or in-store cookery and home economics classes that update grandma's lessons, whether that is how to make stock from discarded bones or program a 21st-century crock-pot.

Cultural cuisine to watch

Today, we are seeing the rise of a new set of cultural influences on flavour and restaurant trends. The move towards humbler, fuss-free fare is seeing simple comfort foods and national cuisines coming to the fore in foodie centres such as London and New York. Street food is coming off the pavement and into the kitchen and eateries.

Wahaca (a phonetic spelling of the gastronomic region of Oaxaca in Mexico) is a restaurant that aims to bring an authentic taste of Mexico to Londoners. The menu is based on market-fresh ingredients, with dishes made to genuine regional recipes and even offering the 'aguas frescas' (fresh waters) that vendors on any Guadalajara street corner whip up from whatever fruit is available.

African and Middle Eastern food is stepping out from the shadow of Moroccan cuisine, and Afghan, Lebanese, and even Ethiopian cuisine are increasingly sought-after. Merkato 55, in New York's trendy Meatpacking District, aims to bring the taste of Africa to Gothamites, with a menu that ranges from Nigerian shrimp fritters and chicken doro wat to Kifto tartare and plantain fufu.

Savvy New Yorkers are discovering the joys of zaatar and mouttabal, thanks to the opening of Ilili in the Flatiron District. Ilili brings a luxurious edge to Lebanese cuisine, with bluefin tuna complemented by mint, parsley and couscous, and Wagyu beef kebabs alongside pomegranate-studded salads and spicy mekanek sausages.

An unfussy approach and honest pricing are key to many of the trends in cultural cuisine, with the added, titillating possibility that diners will uncover an undiscovered culinary culture as the ultimate prize.

SM/ART FO/OD.

'Let food be your medicine,
and medicine be your food.'

_Hippocrates

below | BORBA Skin Balance Water is enhanced with botanicals, antioxidants and vitamins.

SMART FOOD

The phrase '*eat to live*' resonates potently in the pharmacy foods movement. Pharmacy foods, in the guise of functional foods, superfoods and nanofoods, nutraceuticals and nutrigenomics, is still relatively niche; however, this is a food trend which is set to expand, develop and advance over the next 50 years. As consumers' understanding of nutrition has become more sophisticated, they now hope to manage health, performance and appearance by self-medication and the prevention of illness through nutrition.

We already have new hyper-fruit breeds with increased levels of antioxidants, added-value foods, superfood menus and personalised illness-prevention diets. The nutraceuticals industry promotes digestible beauty products and skin '*foods*', and the rapid uptake of this concept proves that consumers are literally buying into the old adage: '*What you put in, you get out*'.

left | RDA Organic Soil Association-approved organic fruit smoothie. The name touts the health benefits, suggesting the serving will provide recommended daily allowance of key vitamins and minerals.

Not on the label

Since the advent of the obesity crisis, brands have been falling over themselves to tout the health-giving properties of their foods, from the addition of nutrients such as Omega-3 fatty acids to yogurt and eggs, to claims about the calcium content in Cheestrings snacks for children. Michael Pollan's book In Defense of Food aims to alert consumers to the spurious health claims made by some food manufacturers. *'Maybe the industry can work out how to make truly healthy convenience foods, but the way they're doing it right now is just pumping up whatever the nutrient of the moment is,'* says Pollan. *'In many cases, when you remove nutrients such as calcium, beta carotene, Omega-3 from their food context, they don't work as well.'*

New EU legislation limits the health claims that food companies can make. Packaging may now only carry claims of improved health and wellbeing if these are based on generally accepted scientific evidence or are well understood by the average consumer.

Obesity futures

The first world's obesity crisis is no secret. In the US, government statistics suggest that Americans now eat 12% more calories a day than in the 80s. As a result, the number of overweight Americans has risen from 47% in the 70s to 66% in 2004.

The impact on health services could be massive: the Foresight report on obesity predicts that this could contribute to a 70% rise in incidences of type-2 diabetes, a 30% rise in strokes and a 20% rise in coronary disease. Fat is now a social and moral issue: 29% of UK consumers feel that those who endanger their own health by overeating should be fined.

The health crisis is even beginning to hit countries that formerly exemplified healthy, pleasurable eating. In Italy, the growing popularity of junkfood over the traditional nutrient-rich Mediterranean diet is contributing to the rise in deaths associated with high-fat diets and 9% of the population is now classed as obese. In response, the Italian government is following the example set in China, sending fruit and vegetables to schools, hospitals and offices, making fruit more widely available in vending machines, and reducing the cost of fresh vegetables. The EU is also taking action and has recently voted to supply free fruit and vegetables by paying farmers to give their surplus produce to schools, hospitals and even holiday camps.

Hyperfoods

Superfoods and health drinks are fast becoming *'hyperfoods'*, which not only improve wellbeing, but also prevent disease and the effects of ageing. A recent study by the World Cancer Research Fund found that certain foods are not merely bad for the waistline, but can actually increase susceptibility to cancer. Processed meats such as ham and bacon can increase the chance of getting cancer by 10% and, while drinking red wine can reduce the likelihood of heart disease, it can increase the possibility of mouth, throat and breast cancers. Rather than giving general advice to eat healthily, we can envisage doctors and governments advising people to eat or avoid specific foods according to the risk of diseases they may be susceptible to.

Consumers' new awareness of the benefits and dangers of certain foods has fuelled the boom in *'superfoods'* and a greater interest in the benefits of micronutrients such as lycopene (found in tomatoes) and Omega-3 fatty acids (found in oily fish). As a result, we are seeing the rise of added-value foods that claim to improve brain function, cholesterol levels or skin condition. It's no longer enough for foods to provide energy, people are now demanding active health benefits, too. According to Euromonitor, the functional foods market is now worth £8.2bn in Japan, while in the UK the market has doubled in the last four years to £2.7bn, dwarfing the UK's £1.9bn organic market.

Historically, products including ingredients with a health effect were related to categories and lines with a healthy image, such as dairy products and fruit juices. But according to Beverage Daily magazine, they are increasingly being incorporated into categories such as biscuits and sweets where manufacturers seek to overcome negative consumer perceptions concerning health. We're now seeing *'skin-balancing'* jelly beans infused

right | Sip flavoured water with beauty benefits.

with açaí berries that are supposed to purify the blood and deliver high doses of antioxidants to the skin, as well as taste-less, powdered supplements that can be added to your vodka martini or coffee or even sprinkled over ice cream to '*cancel out*' any negative effects.

Hyperfoods are now hitting the general health market. Fruit-flow, for example, is a tomato-based extract developed by US-based Provexis, which claims to benefit the heart and blood circulation. The extract is said to inhibit platelet aggregation, part of the blood-clotting process that can cause heart attacks and strokes. Health foods designed for the heart in the US, Japan, Australia and five major European markets are currently worth $3.6bn, according to Leatherhead Food International; but the category is set to expand by 60% over the next five years.

Anti-stress chocolate

We are also seeing the rise of anti-stress foods, filler foods and '*brain foods*'. In Japan, the launch of Glico's Mental Balance chocolate, containing GABA, has been a runaway success, due to its claims that the ingredient GABA (gamma-aminobutyric acid), a neurotransmitter, reduces stress, which appeals to a nation of workaholics. GABA bars now have annual sales of $40m in Japan alone.

Beauty foods

Similarly, we are witnessing the growth of beauty foods in the lifestyle cosmetics sector. Compressed super-ingredients, such as Nutrx8Complex, have appeared in a range of beauty aids

called Skin Appétit. One dose of Nutrx8Complex provides blueberries, cantaloupe, red grapes, yogurt, honey, figs, walnuts and dark cocoa chocolate, together with vitamin B5, vitamin E, macadamia seed oil, vitamin C, aloe and tea tree oil.

Meanwhile, as the market for traditional slimming products tumbles, brands are creating drinks and foods that claim to induce a feeling of fullness so that people eat less, portion control being key to losing weight. Flavourless fibre gels such as Viscofiber are being added to everything from juice drinks and soups to ice cream and biscuits, to promote the feeling of being full without eating too much.

Nanofood

Scientists are now taking the idea of hyperfood even further with the development of nanofoods, products that contain nanoparticles, which can deliver nutrients or even medication on a molecular level. Although much of the development of nanofoods is being kept tightly under wraps, nanotech is a billion-dollar industry: the EU has already contributed £1.7bn to research, while analysts predict the nanofood industry could be worth $20bn annually by 2010.

One of the key developments in nanofood is '*programmable foods*', which enable consumers to decide the exact taste and texture of a product. For example, a can of colourless, flavour-less soft drink would be full of different nanoparticles that could be activated to create the exact colour and flavour you want, as well as adding your chosen nutrients, such as caffeine or Omega-3.

Far from merely creating '*frankenfoods*', nanofoods can help solve long-standing problems such as shelf life and packaging waste. The technology is being applied to smart packaging that can lengthen the shelf life of foods. Undetectable nanofilms

right | Y Water claims to be beneficial for children's growth and development. Each flavour has a name such as Muscle Water, Bone Water, Immune Water and Brain Water. **opposite |** RDA Organic Soil Association-approved organic fruit smoothie. The name touts the health benefits, suggesting the serving will provide recommended daily allowance of key vitamins and minerals.

made of titanium or silicon oxides can kill bacteria and increase the life of many manufactured foods, even when their packaging has been opened, as well as reducing the food industry's massive wastage of plastic packaging.

Small world

Nanotechnology is increasingly being used in a range of foodstuffs already on the market, including Tip Top Up bread and Shemen Industries' Canola Oil. Tip Top Up adds the Omega-3 to a nanocapsule liposome and Shemen uses a nanoformation that reduces cholesterol by competing with the body's bio-system, preventing cholesterol from being absorbed.

'An interesting area for nanotechnology is taking food that's bad for us like chocolate, sugary drinks, chips, and making them good for us,' says Mark Morrison, scientific manager at the Institute of Nanotechnology. A new nanotechnology process is being worked on to remove fat from mayonnaise: solid globules of fat are replaced by liquid nutrients and minerals. The result still

tastes and feels like mayonnaise, yet contains a fraction of the fat. *'The scientific process is actually quite simple,'* says Morrison. *'It's just a case now of getting it to a point where it's cost-effective to reproduce on a mass scale.'*

The potential benefits of edible nanotechnology include:

Removing fat from products such as mayonnaise, without altering the taste, texture or smell

Making oils such as canola and soya not only cholesterol-free but able to reduce cholesterol by competing with the body's natural biosystem

Adding nutrients such as vitamins and minerals to everyday items such as bread, meat, dairy, fruit juice and pasta

Delivering nutrients in a vehicle that protects them from stomach acids

DO-IT-YOURSELF HEALTH

Over the past decade, faith in health services has waned. Excessively long waiting lists, postcode lotteries for drugs, the MRSA *'superbug'* and a series of well-publicised mistakes have compounded this feeling and heightened hospital phobia. This, in turn, has increased the desire to prevent illness and, where possible, self-treat. The market in self-diagnosis equipment is reflecting this desire, with sales of blood pressure, blood glucose and body fat-measuring kits increasing by 30% in the last five years.

Spotlight on health

On both sides of the Atlantic, health and wellbeing has become a major media focus. Consumers are being bombarded with conflicting messages, from scare stories to lifestyle advice. Despite confusion over what is and isn't healthy, for many people the main message that health is influenced by nutrition has hit home. This has fuelled a thirst for genuine, unbiased information on health and nutrition. Websites such as those for the Food and Behaviour Research charitable organisation (Fabresearch), the NHS's Behind the Headlines and the Consumers for Health Choice site are popular, with Fabresearch getting an average of 10,000 visitors every month. Consumers for Health Choice, alone, has a database of over 267,000 supporters.

Diet-linked disease

Media coverage of new research and online information has greatly heightened public understanding of how diet can make the body more susceptible to, or prevent, disease. A recent study by the World Cancer Research Fund stated: '*Evidence shows that vegetables, fruits and other foods containing dietary fibre (such as wholegrains and pulses) may protect against a range of cancers,*' and came with a list of top 10 dietary recommendations to reduce cancer risk.

Last-stop pharmaceuticals

A niche but sizeable demographic is reluctant to turn to pharmaceuticals and instead implements a range of '*natural*' techniques that include homeopathy, Chinese herbal medicine, diet changes and supplement courses. Medicines derived from plant, fruit, seed, and bark extracts are soaring in popularity and courses specialising in treating health through nutrition such as those offered by the College of Natural Nutrition, Raworth International College and the College of Natural Therapy are heavily attended.

Performance eaters

A burgeoning consumer demographic buys foods purely for health-giving properties, without being concerned whether these are organic, pure or natural. These consumers want to look and feel as good as they did in their youth and have no intention of giving in to the signs of ageing. They are fuelling the functional foods market as they not only buy to improve their own wellness, performance and appearance, but also that of their families. For these groups, heightened performance and health is the only goal and if that comes through products with a wealth of added vitamins and minerals subjected to fat- or sugar-stripping processes or synthetic production processes, so be it.

Food medics

Those at the forefront of self-medication through nutrition are the key consumer group driving the pharmacy foods market. They research and hone their knowledge to achieve a diet that maintains and enhances health, performance and function. Consumers in this group are the early adopters of new super/functional foods and innovative food production systems but only if they believe the products have genuine, proven health benefits.

Turning point

Datamonitor figures tells us that the combined US, Western European and Asian-Pacific functional food and drink market is worth $72.3bn, proving that when it comes to health-boosting food, consumers are willing to pay extra. But, according to industry experts, despite impressive sales figures, the functional foods and drinks market is about to enter a '*critical era*'. Although consumers are actively seeking out food and drink that optimise performance and reduce the risk of illness, they are becoming more sceptical about the health claims made by food and drink manufacturers ... a lack of confidence in food and drink with '*artificial*' ingredients means more consumers are opting for naturally healthy diets in order to boost their health.

Super lovers

Although many nutritionists are dismayed at the '*superfoods*' industry because of its hiked-up prices, a niche but affluent and loyal demographic of consumers has seized on superfoods with ardour and is happy to pay premium prices. According to Julian Mellentin, executive director and editor-in-chief of New Nutrition Business, these are '*the over-40s and 20-30-year-old metropolitans who don't know the price of anything.*' Since pomegranates made their grand comeback in 2002, a wealth of other '*superfruits*' has followed, including açaí, blueberry, acerola cherry and boysenberry. Now manufacturers are squeezing superfruits into as diverse a range of products as possible, from tea to beauty products.

'*The success of supposed superfruits shows the magic bullet theory people attached to medicine for so many years is now being attached to individual foods rather than a balanced, varied and colourful diet,*' says Alex Richardson, nutritionist and founder of the Fabresearch heath and nutrition website. '*Consumers want a quick fix, so-called 'superfoods' appear to give it (but in isolation obviously don't) and that's why they're successful.*'

The new superfruits

Superfruits such as açaí, blueberry, pomegranate and acerola cherry, already in a range of teas, beauty products and dairy/fruit combination products, will be increasingly deployed. As these become commonplace, watch out for a new generation of superfruits – cherimoya, mangosteen, luo han guo and the highly nutritious Jamaican naseberry, yet to be widely used.

Beauty foods

Beauty-to-go | The huge success of Borba's beauty enhancing water drinks, crystals and Gummi Bears will herald a rush to make similar beauty boosting confectionery and beverages that are equally appealing, convenient and portable. Borba is currently working on beauty patches that deliver all the nutrients needed to aid optimum beauty with the convenience of a stick-on patch.

Guarana glow | Guarana has long been associated with energy drinks. Industry experts predict that it will be big news in beauty through 2008 and beyond. Italian company Vagheggi is already using guarana in products designed to reduce cellulite and skin blemishes.

Anti-ageing | The naturally occurring anti-ageing properties in food such as fresh salmon, açaí, pomegranate, mangosteen and cherimoya will be used increasingly by the beauty industry. Beauty brands will devise their own diet and nutritional plans, as NV Perricone currently does, aiming at glowing complexions, skin and hair. Dr. Perricone predicts the humble blackcurrant will soon reach superfruit status and will be used in increased numbers of beauty supplements.

Oil us up | Naturally occurring oils such as borage and olive oil will be increasingly used in beauty products due to their high composition of essential acids. Dr. Perricone already has an entire range based on olive oil, including products such as Olive Oil Polyphenols Nutrient Face Fortifier.

opposite from left | Goji & Choklad ningxia berries by Superfruit; Goji ningxia berries by Superfruit. **right** | Magic Fruits beauty snacks.

ADDING VALUE

The market is responding to the demand for pharmafoods with a wealth of products. From enriched chips to cholesterol-reducing crisps and fruits with hyped-up levels of antioxidants, the industry is striving to serve up the general public's health needs on a plate – or via a tablet, bag, wrapper, can or even bottle.

Doctor, doctor

Ironically, as the public steers clear of general practitioners, the red carpet is being rolled out for medics working in food and beauty, with products conceived by '*doctors*' becoming more prevalent on shelves. German brand Dr. Karg's organic crispbreads are rapidly becoming the latest in gourmet, health-boosting crackerbreads, while American beauty brand NV Perricone MD, named for dermatologist Dr. Nicholas Perricone, is receiving accolades for its range of digestible beauty products.

Born-again junk

Manufacturers of traditionally unhealthy foods such as crisps, chocolate, oils and fast food are giving their products a dramatic health makeover. Walkers now fries its crisps in sunseed oil, McDonald's is using organic milk and M&S children's sweets are additive free. American company Corazonas Foods, creator of Corazonas Heart-Healthy Potato Chips, uses a patented technology that infuses plant sterols into the chips. This is claimed to reduce low-density lipoprotein (LDL) cholesterol by up to 15%. Similarly, Israeli firm Shemen Industries has launched Canola Active Oil, also said to reduce cholesterol by using infusions of plant phytosterols.

'*First we had products with lower cholesterol-forming levels. Now we've got products on the market that help lower cholesterol, and in the future there'll be products that stop cholesterol from getting high in the first place,*' says Karl Crawford, business leader of HortResearch in New Zealand, a government-sponsored research programme designed to probe the possibilities of functional food.

Following Corazonas' healthy potato chips, Coca-Cola has brought out a canned green tea drink, Enviga, that burns calories and by 2009 American company Pioneer Hi-Bred International hopes to launch a new soya bean oil that is, through genetic manipulation, healthier and doesn't produce trans fats during cooking.

Omega-3 rush

Many people in countries including the UK, US, Europe and Australia have far too little Omega-3-derived EPA and DHA in their diets, and this has been widely publicised. These essential fatty acids are needed for optimum brain function, and food manufacturers are adding them to anything and everything. McCain has launched a range of Super Crunchy Omega-3 Fries and Healthy Choice Pizzas with added Omega-3, while Heinz has produced Omega-3-enriched tinned Spaghetti Plus, and

Birds Eye has followed suit with Smart Choice Fish Fillets. However, none of these products has set the market alight like Australian bread brand Tip Top Up, an Omega-3-enriched sliced loaf that has become the most popular sliced loaf in the country as it is not only rich in Omega-3, but is deemed perfect '*lunch-box*' size, with a superior grainy taste.

Although generally sceptical of '*added-value*' products and a supporter of nutrients being obtained from their natural sources (fresh fish in the case of Omega-3), Alex Richardson tentatively supports such products. '*Obviously eating [oily] fish twice a week is best, but there is such a massive dearth of Omega-3-derived EPA and DHA that anything healthy that gets it into people's diets is good.*'

Antioxidant take-over

If industry experts are to be believed, antioxidants will become the probiotics of 2008. To date, probiotic drinks are the biggest single market in the functional foods category. Although these are bought by a relatively small number of people, such customers form a dedicated, loyal and repeat-purchasing base. Probiotics, designed to aid the digestive system and boost '*wellness*', have proved a major success for Danone, which produces Actimel, a 1bn brand.

Most consumers, bar the Food Medics group, have an extremely rudimentary grasp of why probiotics are good for them, yet buy into the product anyway. The same goes for the burgeoning interest in antioxidants: consumers purchase products with high antioxidant levels because they see these simply as a '*wellness-boosting*' property. Those with a slightly better understanding may describe antioxidants as compounds that '*kill free radicals, which are, er, bad things we don't want inside us.*'

HortResearch scientists are propagating new strains of apples, kiwis and berries such as raspberry, boysenberry, blackcurrant and blackberry with levels of antioxidants eight times higher than standard crops. They are also looking at the theories about why antioxidants are good for us. '*What antioxidants probably do is signal to cells or activate cells to produce the body's own antioxidants, which help normalise immune function, inflammation and mop up free radicals,*' says Crawford.

---

opposite | Assortment of Organic Crisp Bread by Dr. Karg.

Vita-trends

Although most dedicated health food brands and stores refuse to talk about vitamins and minerals in terms of trends, new products, discoveries and consequent media coverage doesn't mean trends in this sector are as inevitable as in any other. Mintel predicts that major restaurant menu trends for 2008 will include the emergence of *'superspices'*, as *'research is suggesting spices such as cumin, ginger, cinnamon and turmeric may boast more antioxidant power and medicinal benefit than their superfruit cousins.'*

Other trends predicted by Mintel and supported by a wealth of specialist nutrition media, including articles in Functional Ingredients magazine, include a rise in niche grains such as kamut, quinoa, amaranth, barley, millet, groats and teff (strictly speaking the fruit of a herb plant but, due to its form, grouped with grains). These are all easier to digest than wheat, and have greater nutritional value.

---

below | Borba Neutraceutical confectionery claims to contain skin-boosting ingredients. **opposite |** Vitaminwater enhanced with electrolytes and various vitamins.

Super super

As the rush for antioxidant-rich food rises, so will the popularity of superfoods and superfruits – terminology that wasn't introduced into the marketplace until 2005, but which has proved incredibly popular with consumers. In the coming decade, expect a string of new superfruits and herbs that will follow pomegranates, blueberries and blackberries to reach premium price status. A new industry book, Successful Superfruit Strategy: How To Make A Superfruit Business, co-authored by Julian Mellentin and Karl Crawford, advises that a potential new superfruit must have all six of the following characteristics: good sensory properties (taste, colour, feel), novelty, health benefits, convenience and controllable supply and marketability.

As the popularity of superfruits has boomed, both food and nutraceutical manufacturers have begun adding them to a range of products. The Republic of Tea recently launched a seven-strong product line of Superfruit Green Teas, including Açaí Green Tea, Blueberry Green Tea and Acerola Cherry Green Tea.

In the beauty realm, Borba Nutraceuticals, a US company that specialises in nutraceuticals and ingestible beauty products, is using açaí, pomegranate and goji berry in various products that claim to enhance beauty: waters, HD-Illuminating Plasma Infused Crystals and Gummi Bears (yes, Gummi Bears). *'Berries*

are huge right now,' says founder and CEO Scott-Vincent Borba. 'Our products that contain them, especially the Gummi Bears, are extremely popular.' At $25 a bag, Borba Gummi Bears have an almost inconceivable mark-up on standard sweets, yet on their initial launch stockists sold out in just a few days. 'Retailers thought I was crazy, but I saw a gap in the market for ingestible beauty and beauty from within that needed to be filled,' says Borba. 'Borba Nutraceuticals targets problems at the root, inside your body, and it's a concept consumers totally get.'

New and emerging superfruits to look out for include goji berry (going mainstream), mangosteen, guarana, cherimoya, chaste tree berry, luo han guo, noni and the humble blackcurrant.

Target areas

Heart health was targeted by functional food manufacturers during the late 90s via a multitude of 'death marketing' campaigns. Digestive health and weight management will be the key trends of 2008 and beyond. Superfruit author Julian Mellentin believes this is largely because 'digestive health problems from bloating to Irritable Bowel Syndrome affect millions of people and are usually packaged in a general wellness message which is more appealing than products with single-organ appeal.' We can expect to see a rise in foods with added digestive health-improving constituents, such as products from Orafti Active Food Ingredients that feature natural extracts from chicory: inulin, a heterogeneous blend of fructose polymers, and oligofructose, a subgroup of inulin. Sunsweet has produced a beverage called PlumSmart that claims to boost digestive health. In a recent press statement Steve Harris, vice president of marketing at Sunsweet, said: 'With 60 to 70 million Americans suffering from digestive diseases, PlumSmart Light is the only low-sugar juice for digestive health maintenance.' Until another 10 come along...

Natural selection

Within the marketplace we're seeing an increasing trend for isolation of key plant ingredients and enzymes. These are being turned into pure, stand-alone products consumers are hoping will be as effective, if not moreso, as their pharmaceutical counterparts. For example, Pycnogenol is a natural plant extract from the bark of the maritime pine tree which grows exclusively along the coast of southwest France and was billed in Nutritional Neuroscience Journal as relieving symptoms of attention deficit hyperactivity disorder (ADHD) in children.

Lyc-O-Mato is a supplement produced by Israeli company LycoRed, and is derived from tomato lycopene, believed to help prevent free-radical damage to human cells. Each Lyc-O-Mato

Controversial products

Bonsoy | Often referred to as the Rolls-Royce of soya milks by coffee baristas for its smooth appearance and creamy taste. Expect sales to rise as foodies discover its superior taste and the health-conscious realise it is one of the few soya milks that already contains sea vegetables.

Children's health | Products such as Danone's Danimals, smoothies for children with probiotic lactobacillus (LGG), will lead the way in the soon-to-explode children's functional food market. Those interested will feed their offspring the same health-boosting foodstuffs they feed themselves and well-meaning parents will look for quick fixes and easy vehicles for topping up their children's vitamin and mineral intake.

Satiety products | Satiety products such as Slimfast's new Hunger Shot drink and Coca-Cola's calorie burning Enviga will generate fans among those who want to control, maintain and reduce their weight with as little effort as possible. Anything that suppresses the appetite without being too extreme will win dedicated repeat buyers.

Mood foods | Already big in Japan, 'mood foods' that help tackle stress, restlessness, lack of concentration and depression will spread. As the effectiveness of drugs such as Prozac is questioned, more people will look to food and naturally occurring ingredients to improve their moods.

capsule contains four times the lycopene of a regular tomato. In addition to the supplement, the company has developed a range of functional drinks: Summer Delight, enriched with antioxidants, lutein and beta-carotene, and Tomato-on-the-Go beverages. In the cosmeceutical category, the company is currently promoting Lyc-O-Guard, a beverage that is claimed to protect against solar radiation and other free radical generators such as pollution.

_'Functional foods, especially in the form of beverages, will be a household concept in the near future.'

'Functional foods, especially in the form of beverages, will be a household concept in the near future although the skin protection category (cosmeceuticals) has the best chance to overtake lagging sales of snack bars and foods,' predicts Zohar Nir, vice president of product development and scientific affairs at LycoRed. 'This century will be the century of nutrition and the young generation won't be able to shy away from learning nutrition at school, which hopefully will lower the rate of degenerative diseases in the future.'

Future clampdown

The future of the functional foods market is uncertain as it is unclear what can and cannot be classed as 'functional', what type of health claims food can make and how these are to be substantiated. In July 2007, the EU Directive brought in the Nutrition and Health Claims Regulation, designed to set out clearly what health claims manufacturers can and cannot make. The Food Standards Agency (FSA) confirmed that a list of nutritional claims is already in use, but that the health claims list is still being developed by the EU. Its planned implementation begins in January 2009. The FSA refrains from conjecturing how the list may affect the functional foods industry. Will products have to be withdrawn or re-branded? As no one yet knows what measures the EU plans to impose or how these will affect the industry, this is, as Karl Crawford of HortResearch says, 'the $64m dollar question'.

---

below from left | Bonsoy soy drink is a nutrient-rich alternative to milk created by Japanese soy masters using traditional recipes perfected over centuries; Function Drinks, boost your memory and mental acuity with powerful antioxidants. opposite | Pure Inventions pure cocoa drops claim to provide a fast chocolate fix without the calories.

SUPERDIETS

Scientific innovation, coupled with changing consumer attitudes, will see the pharmafoods ideology spread throughout the industry in a variety of forms and guises. The pharmafoods trend is cranking up a gear: from the contradictory proposition of nutrient-rich Big Macs to gene-defying personalised diets in the not-so-distant future.

Move over, fish

The much-publicised need for essential fatty acids is pushing the development of non-fish Omega-3- derived DHA and other essential oils such as ARA suitable for the burgeoning vegetarian and vegan market. Using fermentation technology, US company Martek Biosciences Corporation has developed a DHA product derived from micro-algae (already on shelves as Life'sDHA) and has also extracted ARA oils from fungus. Consumers who experience an unpleasant fishy aftertaste from fish-derived Omega-3 capsules, alongside those who don't eat meat or fish, will look to this type of alternative.

Superfood menus

Already in effect in healthy fast-food chain Leon, the trend for superfood menus is set to spread. The most successful menus will not read like a pharmaceutical pamphlet. They will team sumptuously described fare with appealing promises of detox, wellness and vitality. Health food restaurants are already well established; over the next decade expect eateries to open which boast specific health and beauty properties such as Miami's Afterglo beauty restaurant.

Beauty from within

As programmes become more affordable and well-publicised, the ingestible cosmeceutical industry will explode and will be adopted by mainstream and mid-income consumers. Market leader Borba paved the way with its line of waters, crystalline powders (a more portable version of the water products) and Gummi Bears. The eponymous Dr. Nicholas Perricone of NV Perricone has been hailed as a revolutionary dermatologist and celebrity endorsers include actress Uma Thurman. NV Perricone has an extensive product line ranging from a $560 skin and hair supplement programme down to a free, downloadable *three-day nutritional face lift diet* featuring fresh salmon. Perricone's motto on wrinkles and ageing is '*60% is genetics, 40% is up to you*'.

Second generation GM

Most European countries are experimenting with genetically modified (GM) crops. An article in the Economist reports that the European farmers' lobby Copa-Cogeca has warned that the rising cost of feed could wipe out Europe's livestock unless bans on GMOs are lifted; globally there are currently 114m hectares under GMO cultivation. Unlike early incarnations, the new generation of GMO technology can provide health benefits such as low-cholesterol soya oil. Whether this will sway European consumers has yet to be put to the test.

PHARMA FUTURES

Although some consumers doubt the results of functional foods and are moving towards natural products, the pharmafoods market is only just getting under way. It has the potential for massive innovations and growth if manufacturers continue to focus on the qualities that have already won converts: natural, convenient, gut health, satiety, mood food, brain food, antioxidant-rich and ingestible beauty products.

Health and destiny

As nanotechnology and nutrigenomics become more sophisticated and accurate, nutritional information and knowledge will become the norm. Maintaining health will not be a lifestyle choice, but an expectation. Those that choose to ignore their genetic predispositions or eat unhealthily could be refused insurance policies or medical treatment. As is the principle of many natural nutrition courses, individuals will take control of their own health and wellness and manage it in the same way they do their money, instead of relying on medical *'magic bullets'*.

Nutri-detectives

Consumers' ever-increasing knowledge, not only about diet but about formerly impenetrable lists of food preservatives, chemicals and additives, means manufacturers won't get away with adding cheap junk to foods, or with over-hyped product claims. Because the consumers that are interested in health tend to be both vocal and engaged, it will be essential that manufacturers become cautious about not only what they put into their products but also how they brand and market them in relation to the claims they make.

Health to go

Pharmafood manufacturers will increasingly look to providing health-boosting products as conveniently as possible. Dissolvable food strips with all the nutrients of a meal are a short time away. In an interview posted on the Nutraceuticalworld website, Scott-Vincent Borba predicts convenient superfruits that will not require the eater to dispose of skins and cores, a major contributing factor to the runaway success of blueberries.

Bespoke beauty

As the beauty-from-within market expands, we can expect to see a rise in bespoke ingestible beauty products and regimes. The beauty conscious will have access to bespoke (and highly expensive) skin and hair supplement programmes, lotions and waters, developed in accordance with their genetic make-up, ethnicity, skin type, diet and lifestyle. And as this becomes premium, more mainstream products will be launched to service middle-income beauty buyers.

Junk underbelly

Is there potential for a black market that deals in trans and saturated fat-laced products such as burgers, deep-fried Mars bars, pies, bacon butties, chips, deep-pan pizzas and other processed foods? Will junk food bars become the illegal drinking dens and crack houses of the future? Looking to the future, Mark Morrison of the Insititute of Nanotechnology believes that fast food giants will become very interested in using nanotechnology to *'nutritionally beef up their wares'* and reveals that nanotechnology has the potential to *'go into Star Trek territory'*. Some scientists even suggest that eventually, liposomes could be programmed by radio waves to behave differently depending on the consumer's current nutritional needs.

Raiders of the lost fruits

The demand for superfruits will see buyers plunge deeper into the Amazon rainforest, the Sahara Desert and the Caribbean forest to bring little-known fruits to the wider world. Seeking the opportunity to locate varieties that are new, suitable and desirable to western consumers, the fruit innovation world will become increasingly competitive, with monetary rewards akin to those of the precious stone industry. *'Consumers want fruits that are new, exotic and exciting to their palates. The location of origin and story adds towards validating a superfood's premium price,'* says Karl Crawford, co-author of Superfruit Strategy: How To Make A Superfruit Business.

From soup to nuts

The manufacturing, retailing and marketing of pharmafoods are set to become problematic in the short term, as consumers become increasingly wary of hyper-inflated health and wellness claims. The reasons for this are threefold. A growing number of people in their 20s (along with parents and time-pressed singles) are demanding organic options as standard. Meanwhile, legislation set to dampen down the functional food sector's more extravagant claims is also forcing many brands to retreat from the market. Danone, for example, recently withdrew Danecol from supermarket shelves. More worryingly, recent sales figures for *'functional'* (fortified) foods generally suggest that the market is beginning to slow in terms of growth. And the reasons are simple enough. Shoppers either don't understand the claims being made (who can really explain why or how probiotic yogurts work?) or simply don't believe them. We will need claims to be accurate and provable, as well as believable and pronounceable (bifidus digestivus, anyone?). Transparency has become the big factor in all decisions when it comes to eating because consumers are more savvy. We demand that the claims be true, even if our favourite brands are synthetic.

On the other hand, if claims are accurate and provable, as the sales of products containing Omega-3 fatty acids demonstrate, many people will continue to buy into even those products that are more *'artificial'*. Yes, eating oily fish is the best way to consume Omega-3, but if the alternative is to have a nutritionally inadequate diet, functional foods are a preferable, easy way to get consumers to increase their intake.

But if functional food sales are slowing for the moment, at least until the industry simplifies and clarifies its health and wellness messages, superfoods are taking off. This is particularly true of those with an antioxidant benefit, along with superspices, super-skingestibles (skin creams with added antioxidant qualities), superteas, super-smoothies and super, or smart, waters. On top of this, so-called sacred grains such as millet, teff, barley and groats will rekindle our interest in breads, pastas, breakfast cereals and grain-based bars.

Many brands are now tackling the issue of credibility head on and attempting to make organic products available: nature's stuff and nothing else. Others, however, are accepting that a growing number of young people have no objection to food that is *'synthetically pure'*, containing only beneficial additives. To cater to this group, food producers are creating ranges of nano, GM or hyper-enhanced products that deliberately target a generation which is always on, and will continue to be so for decades to come. Organic is the way to woo and win those in their 30s, 40s and 50s; while for those in their teens and at retirement age, *'pharmafoods'* are a welcome option.

Innovations in ingestion

Drinkable sunscreen | Why spend time slapping on suntan lotion when you can drink it instead? Lyc-O-Guard, one of the lycopene-based, tomato-derived products from Lyc-O-Mato, aims to protect against solar radiation and other free radical donors.

Nutrigenomics | As nutrigenomics become more sophisticated, expect personalised diets to become the norm in the quest to prevent the onset of disease. This trend will be supported by the emerging pharmacogenomics industry.

Healthy junk | Food such as Corazonas' potato chips that actively reduce cholesterol will become standard and this kind of technology will be applied to a variety of junkfoods.

Perfected produce | Through selective breeding technology, the nutritional value of fruit and vegetables, particularly antioxidant levels, will be boosted to levels as much as eight times higher than that of naturally occurring produce. This is possible as researchers now have a more sophisticated knowledge of fruit genetics than ever before.

Health-to-go | Dissolvable strips look set to become the new vehicle for supplement absorption with industry experts listing B12, chromium picolinate, melatonin and possibly coenzyme Q10 (CoQ10) as good examples of ingredients that would be suitable for soluble films.

PACK/ AGING.

'The challenges facing food packaging designers today are not just coming up with ways of protecting, preserving, providing cost effectiveness, brand experience and enjoyment, but how to address issues of sustainability and waste minimisation. The increasing challenge is to think about all of these variables at the same time, longer and harder. We're moving away from a sticking-plaster approach and towards a more holistic one.'

_ Nick Verebelyi, director of 3D branding, Design Bridge

above | Packaging from Nusa kitchen in Clerkenwell, London. Designed by Thirdperson, the range of special winter soups have promotional heat-resistant cardboard sleeves that slot onto existing cups.

FUTUREPAK

Sustainable, convenient, economic, protective, attractive, novel, smart and reactive: What we expect today from the packaging around our food reads like a dating service profile. Over-packaging, however, is an issue sure to get almost everyone hot under the collar. From European directives setting out landfill targets to conservation groups evoking images of plastic debris spoiling pristine beaches, public opinion is firmly set against packaging waste and its contribution to climate change.

Sustainability and conservation concerns are generating the kind of frugal sensibility not seen since the post-war period. However, most consumers are unwilling to compromise their lifestyle demands. They still expect convenience, freshness, security, novelty, speciality and even luxury from packaging. As we have discovered, packaging now has to respond to all these demands, often resulting in trade-offs between materials, energy consumption, disposability and consumer demand. This is giving rise to a host of technological, scientific, systematic and material approaches to design. In the future, the perfect packaging profile could be biogenetic, polymorphous, nanomechanical, techno-organic – and perfectly recyclable.

A little goes a long way

The mantra '*reduce, reuse, recycle*' is not going unnoticed by businesses. Considering the soaring costs of the natural resources and energy needed for the production, construction and transportation of packaging, it's hardly surprising that concepts producing economic benefits as well as environmental ones are continuing to evolve. The drive towards lightweight, down-gauged materials is resulting in increasingly thin, light yet durable substances and ever more efficient processes.

The manufacturers of fast-moving consumer goods (FMCGs) in both Europe and the US are starting to make dramatic savings and boost their green credentials by simply reducing the consumption of raw materials and energy used in packaging. Last year's Container Lite project by the Waste and Resources Action Programme (WRAP), in conjunction with Coors, achieved weight reductions of 13% for the brewer's 300ml Grolsch bottle, saving 4,500 tonnes of glass a year

without any impact on brand perception. Mars has similarly developed a lightweight jar for its Uncle Ben's sauce brand. Heinz has reduced the thickness of the ends of its cans for baked beans and soup by 10%, or 0.02mm. This tiny reduction has brought the company massive savings: 1,400 tonnes of steel and £404k every year, without any change in the appearance of the cans. Even polyethylene terephthalate, or PET, one of the most lightweight and shatterproof synthetic polymers, is being pared back. Earlier this year, Coca-Cola unveiled its lightest PET bottle in conjunction with WRAP, while Innocent Drinks has opted for a 100% recycled PET bottle for its drinks and smoothies.

this page | Stanley Honey, packaging for urban bees honey. The Partners designed this packaging where you re-use the clay plant pot to encourage more honey making in the future.

Tasteful design

In these days of landfill shame and overconsumption, designers are on the hunt for new, environmentally sustainable materials to answer the world's design needs. The solution, it seems, lies in food and the possibilities of edible design pieces. Japanese designer Nosigner's light unit '*Spring Rain*' is made out of bean-starch vermicelli and is edible when boiled. This gives it what Nosigner suggests are perfect environmental credentials: '*Edible products create zero trash*'. Martino Gamper's installation '*Total Trattoria*' aimed to bring people together in a

dining experience supported by design. All elements were custom-created, including low-hung lamps made from delicately rolled flat bread. OKAY studio similarly adopted the food-meets-design theme when transforming the setting for the Brit Insurance Designs of the Year award ceremony. The London-based collective created an innovative series of table centre-pieces, reinterpreting the iconic Anglepoise lamp in bread. French designers Sébastien Cordoleani and Franck Fontana have also turned their talents to tasty materials with a series of sweets currently on sale at Barcelona's Papabubble sweet store. The duo has approached sugar in a similar way to glass, moulding, blowing and stamping it into delightful lollipop shapes. Sugar was also the focus of Oliver Kessler's SugarCubeLight, a giant sugar cube made from a mixture of sugar and resin, which according to Kessler, '*will last for eternity*'.

For Greetje van Helmond, choosing food is a comment on the impermanence of fashion, as opposed to the permanence of the materials used. She chooses food for exactly the opposite reasons to Kessler: for its ephemerality. For her graduate exhibition at the Royal College of Art, she took basic foodstuffs and transformed them into functional or valuable objects, including a wall made out of bread and jewellery made from sugar crystals. '*It fits into the debate about sustainability and in this quest we have to find new materials to work with,*' says van Helmond about her work and the trend towards food as material. '*But for me, it's also about creating something by hand.*' Like other designers, van Helmond is celebrating food as a tactile material. In today's design climate, where so much is done via 3D imaging and rapid prototyping, designers are turning to food because of its hand-crafted, tangible and organic qualities.

above | '*Unsustainable*' necklace by Greetje van Helmond.
below from left | flat bread lamps by Martino Gamper for Total Trattoria at The Aram Gallery; Spring Rain Lamp by Nosigner made from bean starch vermicelli.

Novelty

Although nothing on the supermarket shelves can expire as quickly as a cocktail ring made of sugar, the drive for superior product characteristics and brand differentiation is leading to the development of novel packaging structures, films, inks and printing technologies. Franco Bonadio, chief creative officer of packaging design and branding consultancy Identica, points out that in the premium liquor sector, people are drinking fewer spirits. This means that brands are having to find ways of adding value to the product in order to increase its appeal on the shelf. One way to do this is through seductive packaging.

In terms of novelty, dessert brand Gü caused a storm last year and scooped packaging awards for its original ice-cream container, designed by Big Fish. Gü's black polystyrene cube, while insulating the product and keeping it cooler for longer, was said to exude the aura of a *premium* product.
New York group T-Ink and MWV (MeadWestvaco) are also exploring inventive ways to use printed electronics to foster interactivity between packaging and point-of-purchase dis-

plays. Their recent work for British American Tobacco, creating moving on-pack graphics, has sparked dialogues with premium spirits brands and corporations such as Inbev. Innovative films such as water-soluble and edible MonoSol, which completely bypasses packaging waste, are creeping into flavours, colourants, dyes, vitamin fortifiers and drink mixes. Plastic Logic's flexible electronic greyscale displays and Sony's unprecedented full colour 0.3mm version, are also exciting possibilities, with lightweight, durable properties and potential to provide distinctive labelling and graphics for high-end foods.

above | Sony's flexible, full-colour organic electroluminescent display (OLED) built on organic thin-film transistor (TFT) is only 0.3mm thin and shows 16.7 million colors.

PACKAGING

above | A DEFRA-funded refillable packaging systems project in conjunction with The Boots Company, which aims to investigate the potential for developing refillable packaging systems for body wash products which are more sustainable and appealing to customers. **right |** display module for portable electronic reader devices. Plastic Logic is building the first commercial manufacturing facility targeted at flexible active-matrix display modules for *'take anywhere, read anywhere'* electronic reader products. It will utilise a unique process to fabricate active-matrix backplanes on plastic substrates which, when combined with an electronic-paper frontplane material, will be used to create display modules that are thin, light and robust. This will enable a digital reading experience that is much closer to paper than any other technology. **bottom |** Gü Ice Cream design by bigfish.co.uk. **opposite |** Milk Pouches, Reduce materials use. Carmarthenshire organic dairy co-operative Calon Wen's initiative supplies milk in polythene bags which can be transferred to reusable jugs.

Provenance and freshness

The surge in chilled cabinet food products, led by consumer desire for nutritious and fresher, preservative-free food, is being met by innovations in multilayer barrier materials, breathable films and vapour-permeable resins.

Materials such as DuPont's patented spunbonded semi-permeable polyolefin, Tyvek, are being used to preserve the fresh look of red meat, says AM Associates partner Steve Aldridge. Graham Packaging is also developing what is being touted as the first PET multilayer jar, with barrier properties that can increase the shelf life of pasta sauces, salsas and fruits for up to 12 months.

Perhaps one of the significant developments in barrier packaging is the ongoing research into making PET suitable for packaging beer. Even though PET can behave like a sieve for the oxygen and carbon dioxide in the beer, progressively more sophisticated and thinner multilayer barriers look set to open a whole new market.

Reassurance about the provenance, authenticity and purity of food is fuelling the development of security and anti-counterfeiting technologies such as smart tags and the application of nanomaterials. Nanomaterials vary from extremely lightweight and invisible coatings that can detect pathogens to nanofillers that can delay food spoilage through a range of physical and chemical barriers and processes. Developments in nanotechnology that take the form of inconspicuous nanotubes and particles embedded in packaging or labels can also respond to security sensors.

Back to basics

The difficulty of recycling plastics in the US is renewing interest in traditional materials such as glass and metal, says Rider Thompson, founder and editor of online sustainable packaging publication, Sustainable is Good. *'Due to the exponential growth of PET, glass is now becoming a way to stand out,'* he explains. *'We're seeing designers once again considering glass in the water industry and there is continued strong use of glass packaging in the premium soda markets.'* While glass is heavier than PET and consumes more transit fuel, it is more easily recycled and tends to signify a premium brand in the minds of shoppers.

The perfect plastic

The compromise between the sustainability and carbon footprint of materials that are easily recycled but heavy and energy-consuming to transport, and lightweight synthetics, easily produced but difficult to degrade, is causing manufacturers and designers to explore new types of synthetic materials.

These are designed to be lighter, consume less energy, and offer superior barrier properties, rigidity, flexibility and durability, thus addressing the sustainability conundrum. The most lightweight of all thermoplastics, cutting-edge polypropylene (PP) and polyolefins, produced by European manufacturers including Borealis and Basell, under the Stretchene brand, feature advanced weight reduction. PP density is 34% lower than PET density and it outperforms PET in terms of rigidity and water vapour transmission rate. As a result, Unilever South Africa Foods recently opted for Milliken & Company's Millad® PP format rather than PET for its Robertsons spice range. The US dairy sector has also been quick to embrace PP, despite a dearth of recycling facilities, says Thompson. Stonyfield Farm has led the way, with nearly all yogurt manufacturers following suit. In fact, says Thompson, '*most in-house grocery store brands are now using PP.*'

Designers are also seeing the advantages of improved, efficient lightweight synthetics. Champions include US-based industrial designer Karim Rashid who admits: '*I always find myself defending plastics. I read recently that despite the fact that plastic plays a role in every aspect of our daily lives, its production accounts for only 4% of US energy consumption. The real answer to the use of plastic is that we should use less, and use it better.*'

_ '*The design challenge is really about understanding both consumer and business needs.*'

Going, going, almost gone

Because of the huge infrastructure investment needed to develop new packaging, designers are also looking for logical, simple ways to reduce transit packaging and energy consumption. Design consultancy SeymourPowell has been working with a number of FMCG brands on the development of new product formats that take up less space and consume less transit energy. Co-founder Richard Seymour says that by rethinking product formats, looking at reduction of water volume, concentrates and compact products, significant environmental and economic savings can be made without any major impact on manufacturing methods or existing infrastructure. For example, US brand Welch's, which produces a concentrated juice packaged in a plastic 'can', has achieved a 75% reduction in packaging by simply not shipping water.

Bioplastics and biodegradable plastics

Innocent is a widely known beacon of brand power in the marketing world. It's little wonder that the company's 2004 foray into cornstarch bottles, helped by Pearlfisher's Innovation Scout programme, has stimulated interest in the bioplastics market. Because biopolymers revert back to organic material when composted correctly, early biopolymers were quickly touted as the way to lessen the impact of disposable packaging and the burgeoning plastic landfill expected to outlast our children.

Bioplastics, ranging from glossy, transparent polylactic acid (PLA) to palm fibre, reed fibre, bamboo and PlasTerra offer good printability, without pre-treatment. Certain types, in particular starch-based polymers, feature aroma or fat barriers and high oxygen barrier properties. They also have a pleasing surface texture, anti-static properties and a great capacity to withstand impact. Boots packages its sandwiches in cardboard with PLA windows, while organic food brand Fresh! Naturally Organic, uses Nature Green PLA containers for its salads and a biodegradable Tecta board for its sandwiches.

Continuing research in the field is yielding further developments. Scientists from the National Institute for Agro-Environmental Sciences in Japan have reported the discovery of yeast that can disintegrate degradable plastics, producing a fibre-rich pulp. *'We're looking at using material that is a byproduct of the production of sugar beet for our new pie range,'* says a spokesman for Fresh! Naturally Organic. *'This is great, because it would only be wasted otherwise.'*

Current debate about landfill, which might spoil virgin forest or land which could otherwise be used for food production, poses an ethical dilemma for many packaging designers. This is leading to the development of plastic additives that trigger a much quicker, *'natural'* breakdown of synthetically produced polymers when added during extrusion in the manufacturing process. Interest is growing in new formulas such as Begg & Co's Bio-Batch and Symphony's d2w.

Probably the most exciting biopolymer development, however, is that of photovoltaic biopolymers. Produced by BioSolar, the *'bio back sheet'* can be used in photovoltaic cells, posing possibilities for portable power, without emissions.

The major issue surrounding biopolymers, however, centres on concerns over contamination of the synthetic recycling chain and confusion over composting guidelines. Some require commercial composting while facilities aren't always readily available. Last November, Innocent Drinks scrapped the NatureWorks cornstarch PLA it had introduced for its smoothie bottles because it said the material did not use any recycled content and local commercial composting was not yet a mainstream option. Rider Thompson points out that, although the US has been slower than Europe to embrace biopolymers, petroleum-based fresh produce trays in America are starting to be replaced by containers made of palm fibres. Earthcycle, one of the major US suppliers, is now providing palm fibre packaging to retailers such as Wal-Mart, Publix, Safeway, Loblaws, Kroger and Wegmans.

Steve Aldridge of AM Associates suggests that bioplastics are probably the best option where there are currently no or few recycling opportunities. The challenge ahead for designers, manufacturers and suppliers appears to be the development of better standards to describe degradability, the source of raw materials, and composting directions.

Re-usability

Once a familiar scene, but now a rarity in the UK, the milk round, with its 'service-design' approach and environmental, economic and social benefits is beginning to inspire designers who are exploring packaging systems based on reusability. Across Europe, it is normal practice in countries such as Germany and the Netherlands to return glass bottles and retrieve a deposit paid, proving that misconceptions of poor quality and delivery can be overcome. Dutch retailer Albert Heijn currently runs a closed loop and reusable system for Coca-Cola Light and natural mineral water 1.5l refillable PET bottles, with bottles lasting up to 20 trips. Canadian retailer The Big Carrot operates a similar system for Harmony Organic milk. Customers buy a 500ml refillable milk bottle in-store and pay an extra deposit of about 70p at the till. Empty, rinsed bottles are returned to the store for bulk collection. The US organic chain Whole Foods Market runs a number of dry foods refillable systems; consumers bring their own storage boxes and fill them from large containers in-store.

Dr. Vicky Lofthouse, design and technology lecturer at Loughborough University, has completed a two-year Defra-funded project on refillable packaging systems with Boots for its Botanics bodywash range. Lofthouse is now preparing her research for food applications and is receiving expressions of interest from supermarkets such as Tesco. The many considera-

tions in designing refillable packaging systems, including branding, economic and consumer concerns, make for a time-consuming and complex process. This intricacy has hindered their acceptance, according to Lofthouse. While consumers may be happy to invest in an expensive dispenser, this doesn't necessarily guarantee that they will continue to buy that particular brand. Compatibility between systems could mean they choose a cheaper refill, says Lofthouse. These are major concerns for brands researching this type of packaging option. Once consumers have been assured of good quality and delivery, however, it can be a good way of locking them in, especially if a price incentive is offered. So far, Lofthouse has matched several food categories to suitable refillable types: concentrates concepts could be applied to products like the Nescafé Espresso ranges, dispensing systems that could be adapted for water and soft drinks, while door-to-door glass bottle deliveries could see the revival of the milk round.

Designers outside of packaging and food are also getting in on the act, creating beautiful re-usable containers. Design Academy Eindhoven graduate Liora Rosin's collection of delicate, tactile salt shakers is designed around the ritual of filling and emptying, making the refilling process as important as using them.

'The design challenge is really about understanding both consumer and business needs,' says Lofthouse. *'The perception of refillable systems up until we did this project was that they didn't work, but we're now hearing positive noises from industry and business looking to explore how various types of systems can be adapted for particular products.'*

---

opposite from left | Picnick's disposable take-out containers, cutlery, cups, and labels are all biocompostable and biodegradable. made from biodegradable bioplastics and paper. They are derived from renewable raw materials such as starch cellulose, soy protein, lactic acid, etc., which decompose back to carbon dioxide, water, biomass, etc. Picnick also uses 100% biodegradable labels made from renewable resources; Pooch & Mutt products include only natural ingredients and are presented in fully compostable packaging produced from the world's only biodegradable polymer; All innocent smoothies are now packaged in 100% recycled PET plastic.

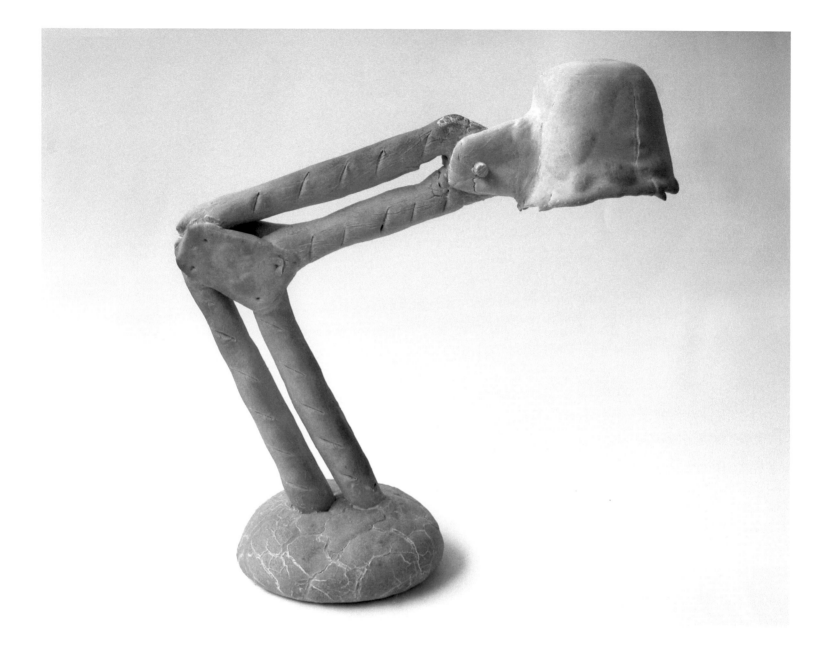

Smart packaging

Technologies evolving from smart packaging, or materials that can respond to a product's environment, are enhancing functionality for both consumers and the supply chain. These technologies allow products to react to changes such as pH value, temperature or pressure. On the consumer side, we're seeing the commercialisation of innovations such as Zeo-Tech's self-cooling beer kegs, which make it possible to drink cool beer anywhere, or self-heating coffee containers by both OnTech and Sonoco, which have been picked up by Wolfgang Puck. Chef Jay's Food Products, available in the US, use a similar exothermic chemical technology for self-heating soup.

European packaging manufacturer Stora Enso has just unveiled CDM Sinuate, a primary and secondary packaging concept that works on the principle of electrical delamination. Originally developed for attaching equipment to the outside of aircraft carriers, this technology now enables boxes to be fixed neatly together, sealed and then re-opened with just an electrical current. Matthew Falla, designer and founder of Osmotronic, feels that developments in smart packaging technology will provide more efficient ways of shopping for food. Radio-frequency identification and near field communication technologies integrated into food labels that connect and respond to mobile phones will also offer consumers the possibility of re-ordering food and stocking up while on the go.

above | Bread Anglepoise lamp by Tomás Alonso, part of OKAY studio

Secondary functionality

As reusables are promoted as the way forward, designers are looking at ways of shifting packaging away from the notion of disposability. Designers Karim Rashid and Matthew Falla have both been working on designs for packaging with secondary uses. Rashid's recent packaging design for Issey Miyake perfume doubles as a travel case, while Falla's Mobipak system, which combines electronic printing with cardboard packaging, allows users to set up their phones by touching printed *'buttons'* on the surface of the pack. Falla believes these principles will migrate to the food-packaging sector, albeit at the luxury end. *'Because of the cost and effort in implementing this sort of packaging,'* he says, *'there needs to be some sort of product or service associated with the packaging to justify it.'*

Aesthetics: natural to the touch

The evocation of wholesome, nutritious and fresh food will continue to be paramount to the look and style of food packaging, says Pearlfisher's realisation director Darren Foley. Uncoated, untreated and unglossy surfaces help consumers to filter out processed products, says Foley. Matt and natural textures, natural fibres, traditional block printing, die-cut card, clear doy packs, minimal patterns and muted colours will continue to be the key graphical ways to communicate uncontaminated, unprocessed food produce on the package. Award-winning

packaging graphics exemplify this trend. For example, those designed by Big Fish for Dorset Cereals have convenient box size and cut-out sections to reveal the texture and visual appeal of the product. The natural touch and feel, Foley says, is one of the ways that designers are attempting to communicate the *'inherent goodness'* of food brands.

From soup to nuts

Packaging has three straightforward functions: to protect, to preserve and to promote. As we become less throwaway in our attitude towards purchases, from food to fashion to FMCGs, packaging will have to strike a difficult balance between conflicting agendas. The first requires prioritising the perceived quality or value of the offer to assure the consumer that the product is worth the attention and the expense; the second requires the communication of a message of reduced costs and resources that will fit with an increasingly environmentally aware mindset.

In the food sector, the pressure is already more intense than in any other. Sizeable reductions in both the amount of packaging used and the energy and resources consumed in creating it are becoming crucial. Free plastic carrier bags in supermarkets will soon be a thing of the past. It will be up to the company to address the quandary that we may want to buy less but we still seek better value and will still demand products that look luxurious and high-quality.

It is encouraging to note that packaging is undergoing seismic technological change – even for taken-for-granted materials such as aluminium and glass. This means all stages of the packaging process will be rethought, from the bottom up. Simple solutions such as lighter-weight cans are a straightforward start; more revolutionary food preservation systems such as pathogen-spotting nanocoatings and digital best-before labels are no longer blue-sky ideas.

Shoppers feel empowered to act on these issues themselves. Citizen action is the order of the day, as we all learn to *'do our bit'*. The ethic, whereby recycling means re-using rather than expecting someone else to deal with the problem, is a growing trend that will see the public expecting food retailers and brands to offer unpackaged food more often. It will be up to the retailer or the manufacturer to solve the health and preservation issues. It has become clear to the wisest food businesses that now is not the time for short-term solutions. Given the stratospheric price rise of many basic food products due to increased costs and demand, it will be incumbent on all producers, manufacturers, processors and retailers to invest in long-term solutions that deliver healthy, value-for-money food in a safe, cost-effective and sustainable manner. To the benefit of all.

opposite | Eggshells, which is the natural packaging of the ingredients has been reused as a mould for the final product–pudding by Cocoro No Akari. **from left** | Stamp. Disposable/reusable cutlery by Tomás Alonso. The form not only gives structural strength, but also allows the pieces to stack as a set or within themselves for storage and transport; Form by Charles Job for Normann Copenhagen.
below | Innovative recycled packaging exhibited at Eat Drink Design, an initiative by design studio Moon/en/co and the culinary phenomenon Sot-l y-laisse, in which eight designers were coupled with eight top-class restaurants during Dutch Design Week.

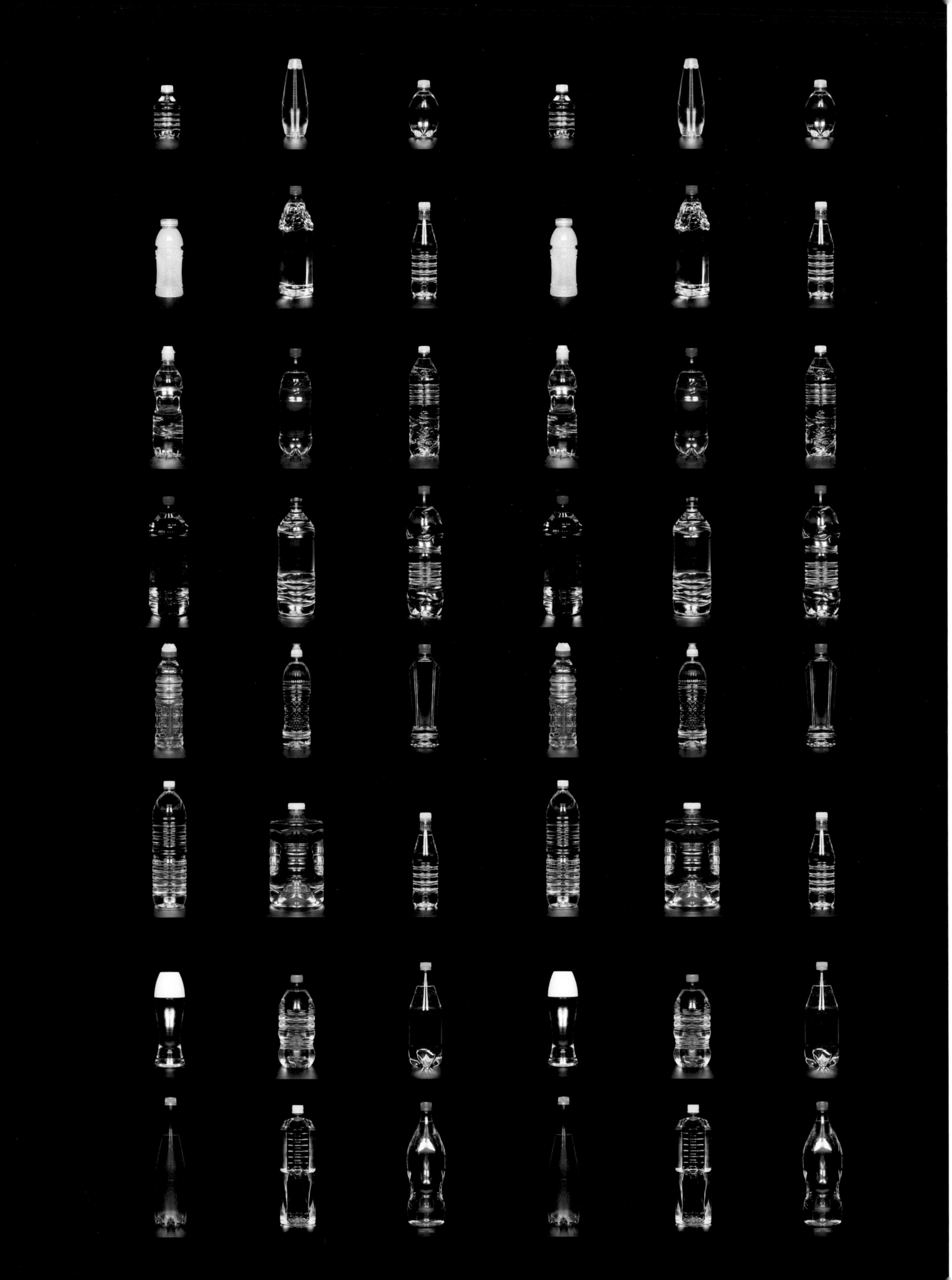

PACKAG /
ING &
POLITICS:
WATER

Tapped out

Bottled water has become big business. Global consumption has grown to 180bn litres per year, up from 78bn in 1998, according to food and drink consultants Zenith International. The BBC program Bottled Water: Who Needs It? examined the environmental aspect of bottled water, calculating that a litre of French mineral water can generate up to 600 times more CO2 than a litre of Thames tap water. This no longer fits with consumer concern over carbon footprints.

Bottled water's wild popularity has hit a wall of eco, food-mile and NuAusterity concerns. Consumers, newspapers and government departments alike are wading in to the tap-versus-bottled water debate. Alongside the eco-issue is a financial one. City governments in the US are turning away from bottled water for both financial and environmental reasons. The US moves 1bn bottles around every week, equivalent to 37,800 18-wheelers delivering water, according to FastCompany magazine. Chicago has started taxing bottled water and San Francisco and Seattle have stopped buying it, trumpeting the quality of their municipal water supply. In each case, it's a great way to save money. The city of Seattle, for example, will save $58k each year. '*Bottled water is good for cycling or when you're at a train station,*' says Consumer Council for Water (CCW) communications officer Amy Weiser. '*But it's not necessary in a restaurant.*' The CCW launched a campaign in February to encourage restaurants to serve free tap water – which, Weiser points out, consumers have already paid for by contributing to infrastructure. They want restaurants not to frown on people whose reply to '*still or sparkling?*' is '*tap*'.

To bring extra chic to the trend, Paris's municipal water suppliers, Eau de Paris, distributed 30,000 carafes designed by Pierre Cardin to convince Parisians that tap is as good as bottled. Meanwhile, US homewares retailer Pottery Barn has started

selling aluminum reusable water bottles in its stores, alongside a sign saying: '*An untold amount of disposable cups and plastic lids are used and discarded every day. Contribute to a healthy environment by choosing a reusable travel mug, drink bottle, or lunch bag.*' Consumers are turning away from overpriced products that they don't need and that damage the environment. In terms of water, this means the tide is turning against bottles.

The renaissance of tap

At a time when London hotel Claridge's has launched a water menu featuring waters sourced from volcanic rock, melted icebergs and the Hawaiian deep seas, costing up to £50 a litre, we are seeing a growing backlash against the waste and environmental damage created by bottled waters. Globally, we consumed 187bn litres of bottled water in 2006, a 7.6% increase on the previous year. It takes 17m barrels of oil to produce the bottles used by Americans for water annually – enough to power a million cars for a year.

Interestingly, in taste tests, tap water regularly scores highly. In a recent blind taste test carried out by Decanter magazine, tap water came third out of twenty-four, behind only Waiwera and Vittel. Why then, are we drinking so much bottled water? In an investigation into '*ripoff mineral water*' the National Consumer Council found that 20% of consumers are too nervous or scared to ask for tap water in restaurants. In San Francisco, restaurants Incanto and Poggio pioneered the serving of filtered tap water five years ago, and civic staff cannot use public money for bottled water. Now other restaurants in California and New York have followed suit. In Paris, tap water is served from Pierre Cardin carafes.

Virtual water actually dirty: David de Rothschild

Virtual water is the amount of water that is needed in manufacturing and food production. In 2006, economists estimated the world's annual virtual water trade to be 1,000 cubic km, or the equivalent of twenty Nile rivers. In 2008, adventurer and environmentalist David de Rothschild built the Plastiki, a raft made entirely of plastic bottles and other recycled materials in order to sail from the US to Australia to draw attention to the consumer dependency on plastic. His route took him through the so-called Eastern Garbage Patch, a rubbish-strewn area of the Pacific Ocean that has accumulated rubbish and flotsam that has been estimated to be larger than, and perhaps even twice as vast as, the continental United States. In 1999, researchers counted a million pieces of plastic per square mile. It has been described by one scientist as a '*plastic soup*'.

---

opposite page | Bottled water as pictured by San Francisco-based fine art photographer Frank Yamrus in a limited edition of 11. '*There are over 3000 brands of bottled water worldwide*', Yamrus says. '*Just 30 years ago commercially produced bottled water barely existed in the United States. Today, Americans are the leading consumers of bottled water at 32 billion litres per year*'.

PACKAG / ING & POLITICS: BAGGING IT

Unpackaged

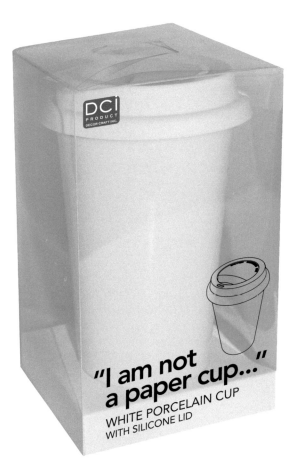

The consumer backlash against plastic bags is extending to all packaging. Retailers are encouraging consumers to bring their own food containers, while designers are creating containers that are more aesthetically pleasing than back-of-the-cupboard Tupperware. The London store Unpackaged offers unpackaged pulses, dried fruits, rice and pasta, herbs and spices, loose sweets and even eco-household cleaners for customers to put into their own containers. All the products are organic or Fairtrade, and if customers don't have enough containers, they can buy re-usable ones in-store. Founder Catherine Conway also runs Unpackaged stalls in chic London street markets such as Broadway Market. UK supermarkets Waitrose, Tesco and Morrisons have introduced 'unpackaged' milk, which aims to reduce packaging by 75%. The milk is sold in one-litre Eco Pak bags made from low-density polyethylene, and decanted at home into reusable, recyclable plastic eco-jugs. According to Calon Wen, which supplies Waitrose, this could reduce the amount of plastic used for milk packaging by 100,000 tonnes every year. Meanwhile, Décor Craft Inc. has introduced the 'I am not a paper cup' porcelain cup, intended to take the place of the plastic and paper cups used by many coffee shops. The double-walled thermal cup and silicon lid are a witty take on the ubiquitous latte cup, which can be filled at coffee shops with your favourite brew, then washed and reused during the next caffeine fix.

'I'm not a plastic bag'

Governments and local authorities are turning against the plastic bag. In Maharashtra State in India, some local councils have banned the production and use of ultra-thin plastic bags. China, too, has done this, leading to the closure of the factories that manufactured them. *'Packaging manufacturers are having to*

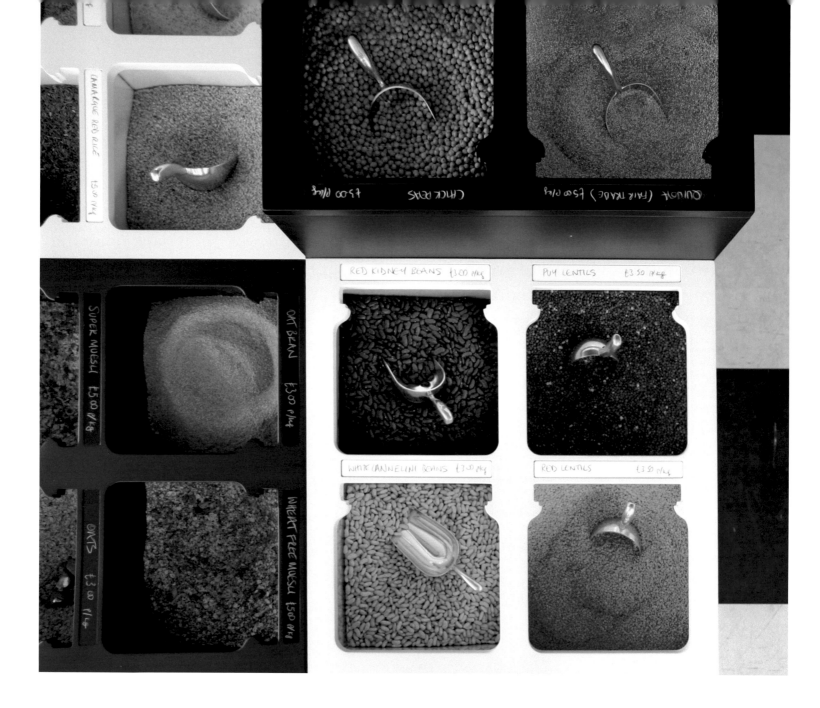

The following labels appear within the image: LINMALIQUE RED RICE £5.00 p/kg · CHICK PEAS £3.00 p/kg · QUINOA (FAIR TRADE) £5.00 p/kg · SUPER MUESLI £5.00 p/kg · OAT BRAN £3.00 p/kg · OATS £3.00 p/kg · WHEAT FREE MUESLI £5.00 p/kg · RED KIDNEY BEANS £3.00 p/kg · PUY LENTILS £3.50 p/kg · WHITE CANNELLINI BEANS £3.00 p/kg · RED LENTILS £3.50 p/kg

cope with the rising price of raw materials and transport, so it is in their interest to keep packaging amounts down,' says Gordon Carson, editor of Packaging News. The Co-op supermarket is planning to redesign its own brand of wine bottles, to save 450m tonnes of glass a year. The French brand Danone has granted the University of Belfast £2.5m to research ways in which nanotechnology could be used to create lighter packaging. Sainsbury's is launching a collection of clothes made of recycled plastic packaging, including soft drink bottles, fruit and vegetable packaging and even meat trays. However, Carson feels that the government and media are misleading the public over packaging. 'Addressing recycling infrastructure is a more pressing issue than recycling, as most recyclable packaging ends up in landfill.'

Packaging news

Consumers have begun to complain that retailers use too much packaging on their products and over half feel that all packaging materials should be easy to recycle. Packaging, or lack of it, is definitely on the consumer agenda today. The plastic milk bottle could be replaced by pouches, which use 75% less plastic. Consumers then fill a jug at home, similar to the way that water filters are used. Pouches are also being considered by wine industry innovators, including Arniston Bay. The growth of stand-up pouches has risen to 99.2m units in Western Europe. And pouches, being lighter, are also cheaper to transport. It would be refreshing to see this innovative approach being adopted by mainstream retailers, but will it?

opposite page clockwise from left | Salt shakers by Liora Rosin; *'I am not a paper cup'* by Decor Craft Inc. **above |** Unpackaged store, London.

PACKAGING

7 | Maisen's sweet sauce, Japan
8 | Nootines dry lentils, Russia
9 | Vedett beer, Belgium
10 | Arroz SOS rice, Spain
11 | Wilhelmina Pepermunt peppermint sweets, Holland
12 | Rindfleisch canned beef, Germany

A MESSAGE ON THE BOTTLE

Message

In recent years, the use of plastic windows in packaging has become a way to assure the consumer that the food inside is just what he thinks it is by revealing the actual contents. A trust-building tool as well as an additional graphic device, this WHAT YOU SEE IS WHAT YOU GET communication has become increasingly important at a time when savvier shoppers want to know more than just what cut of beef they're buying and no longer want to take the retailer's word for it; they want to see the colour, texture and quality of their food with their own eyes.

Colour and materials

Along with this literal and figurative new transparency, no smart food producer will let the chance go by to communicate with the consumer from the shelf. The wrapping should say it all, and does. Natural undyed cardboards convey the message that what is inside is as good for the earth as it is for the body. Fluorescent colours indicate the reverse.

below | Range of mustards for Waitrose Ltd. and Selfridges & Co Smoked Salmon by Lewis Moberly.   right from top | Products by Migros, a chain of food retailers in Switzerland. Their range of gourmet food called Sélection was designed by Schneiter Meier Külling.

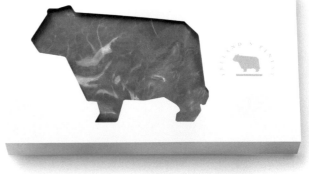

TYPOGRAPHY

Message

Ultra-clean labelling suggests product purity, as well as giving instant shelf appeal in crowded retail environments. These products have a straight-talking '*does what it says on the tin*' approach that fosters an air of honesty and cultivates consumers' trust. With the growth of added-value and traffic-light labelling, these simple designs are a breath of fresh air on crowded shelves.

1 | LÄRABAR pecan pie bar, USA
2 | ÁN/2 red wine, Spain
3 | KUB OR, stock cubes, Nestlé, France
4 | Viel Erfolg honey vodka, Michelsen, Germany
5 | So!Go pure lemon juice, South Africa

Colour and materials

Beautiful, bold typography in rich colours. A modernist style in a limited palette with a maximum of four colours is a basic approach with optimum impact.

1 |

3 |

2 |

4 |

5 |

from above | Range of Waitrose Cooks' Ingredients designed by Christian Stacey and Mary Lewis; Dada 1 Wine Label front and carton designed by Inhouse Design; Stories, a new café concept developed by BVD in cooperation with Ivan Akibar Arkitekter. BVD created a totally unique café experience: from concept and name, to graphic profile and packaging.

PACKAGING

clockwise from left | Logan Wine, a small, family, boutique winery. War Design produced branding through to packaging; Tapio designed by Transfer Studio; Sparky Brand by Williams Murray Hamm; Blossa årgångsglögg (vintage mulled wine). It is launched every year with a new flavour and design. Designed by BVD.

6 | La Molina chocolate, Italy
7 | O&Co (Oliviers & Co) bell pepper and
ricotta cheese pesto, Italy
8 | O&Co (Oliviers & Co) eggplant paste, Italy
9 | Kromland Farm tea, South Africa
10 | Salmiak Pastillen liquorice pastilles, Germany
11 | Eittsett milk chocolate with liquorice, Iceland
12 | Soup, Lafayette Gourmet, France

ZENO

Message

The Zeno trend celebrates all things synthetic. Fluorescent acid brights enhance the youth appeal of candy, energy drinks and snacks. Graphic pattern and innovative shapes unashamedly boast the additives, colours and preservatives within.

Colour and materials

Colours not naturally found in foods, such as bright blue and scarlet, further emphasise these products' artificial contents. Sans serif typefaces simplify the brand message, as well as hinting at the novelty of the product inside – there's no room for nostalgia here.

clockwise from above | dq Vodka; KOR Water hired RKS to create the KOR ONE – a healthy, sustainable, way to stay hydrated; range of Motley Bird.

1 | Kasugai jelly sweets, Japan
2 | Vinzenzmurr frankfurter, Germany
3 | Meiji fudge dice sweets, Japan
4 | Y Water, US
5 | Nói S'r'us Opal liquorice sweets, Iceland
6 | Gajol liquorice sweets, Denmark
7 | Block chocolate bar, Germany
8 | Tohato caramel crisps, Japan

PACKAGING

9 | Bloomsberry & Co chocolate, US
10 | Meiji sweets, Japan
11 | Edomurasaki seasoned seaweed, Japan
12 | Pocari Sweat energy drink, Japan
13 | Kosher Parve sweets, US
14 | Sirop, dilutable syrup, France

9 |

10 |

11 |

12 |

13 |

14 |

| 14

clockwise from above | Fat Pig Chocolate, designed by NY-based The Brooklyn Brothers; Milk packaging sure to get noticed on the shelf. Available in skim, chocolate, and whole. A student work by Ashley Linnenbank; Eye Candy by Beta Tank designed by The Play Coalition. Mixing candy and electronics in the form of a grid or a USB connection is not the most intuitive combination. But we know that the brain can process visual images through other organs besides just the eyes. The tongue, with its concentration of nerve endings and saliva, is particularly adept at receiving electronic stimuli and passing them onto the brain. This means that, with a fine electronic grid placed on the tongue, a person could suck on the sweet or lollipop and see beautiful explosions of colour. This is the intention of Eye candy. The Play Coalition knows that although this pleasure may seem trivial, it is far from unreasonable: *'By rethinking and reclassifying the way we approach technology and the senses,' he says, 'we can be more imaginative and constructive in the way we envision future possibilities.'* The models displayed at MoMA New York's Design and the Elastic Mind exhibition in 2008 were deliberately intended to invite just such a change of approach.

PACKAGING

1 | Dosenbo-chaho organic green tea, Japan
2 | Courier Coffee Roasters coffee beans, US
3 | Summerbird creamy chocolate spread, Denmark
4 | Duskin apple juice, UK

RAW

Message

The unrefined touch of the packaging is as important as the aesthetic with this trend. Pared-down typefaces suggest a traditional, heritage brand, suggesting trustworthiness and value. The unprocessed, handmade feel of the packaging suggests the care and attention given to an artisan product.

Colour and materials

Uncoated cardboards, unbleached papers and traditional materials such as glass create a wholesome image. Matte textures and natural fibres reflect the natural, nutritious contents inside, brightened and modernised with one or two accent colours. Minimal patterning and neutral palettes allude to the simple ingredients and straightforward recipes within.

from above | Range of Sivaris Rice by Pepe Gimeno; Earthcycle™ is a new packaging approach using only renewable and compostable materials. The EarthCycle™ tray is made from palm fibre, a renewable resource, which would otherwise be a waste product; The Natureflex™ film is sourced from renewable resources. The label is also certified home compostable; 'Proef Beans', more or less a fun project by Marije Vogelzang; Pooch & Mutt products include only natural ingredients and are presented in fully compostable packaging produced from the world's only biodegradable polymer.

clockwise from above | Sheila's by Company, a design studio based in London. A labeling system for a cottage industry that makes seasonal jams, marmalades and chutneys. Company created a label for each ingredient (defined by the ingredient colour) and months of the year, to reflect the fact that recipes and ingredients change with the seasons; Fabric that is sewed on gift box from Mutterland (Mother country) from Germany; Mutterland's own range of tea; Askinosie Chocolate is a small batch chocolate manufacturer located in Springfield, Missouri, sourcing 100% of their beans directly from the farmers. The Askinosie Chocolate mission is to serve their farmers, their neighbourhood, their customers and each other.

5 | TRUEfoods beef stock, UK
6 | Conscious chocolate, UK
7 | Erich Hamann chocolate, Germany
8 | McKenzie's biscuits, Scotland
9 | Egadi sea salt, Italy
10 | Georges Bruck goose fat, France

5 |

6 |

7 |

8 |

9 |

10 |

PACKAGING

clockwise from above | Raise them on Robinsons. One of a series of 14 posters for Robinsons by Adrian Johnson; Duoido designed a Unisex T-shirt inside a milk-like shaped pack. Serie II is limited. 300 units each one. Pack made of 1 special type of ink, fluo. 2 print design patterns were developed on two colored cotton jersey; Melt, a gourmet chocolate shop, plays with the characteristics of melted chocolate in its logo and packaging in a fun and sophisticated way. The bar's patterns look as if they were illustrated with chocolate while the tins have the look of being dipped by Jesse Kirsch.

6 | The Fine Cheese Company biscuits, UK
7 | Tohato green pea crisps, Japan
8 | Laurelwood Brewing Co. ale, US
9 | Happy Monkey açaí juice, UK
10 | Artisan Biscuits organic biscuits, UK

FO/OD SPA/CES.

From luxurious canteens and cooking laboratories to superduper markets and pudding palaces, an introduction to the designers, concepts and interior design approaches that are changing restaurant, supermarket and store design.

FOOD SPACES

Superduper Markets

Supermarkets around the world are turning to design to defy the homogenised hell of the suburban identikit. At Eataly in Turin, a former vermouth factory has been converted into a vast food market offering an array of artisanal produce from around Italy. Each department contains its own restaurant where specialist chefs create mouth-watering seasonal dishes from Eataly produce. The cavernous space houses numerous cafes and bars where enthusiasts can learn about wine and beers or the importance of seasonal food. They can also explore the Eataly library or attend cooking classes.

Austrian supermarket chain MPreis uses stylish architecture and interior design to position itself as a 'sexy supermarket'. Since 1993, the company has commissioned up-and-coming architects to design stores inspired by their Alpine environment. The store in Innsbruck, designed by local Rainer Köberl, features elegant lighting, glacial ceiling panels and artfully displayed fresh produce.

Manhattan's favourite luxe supermarket Dean & DeLuca is expanding into the Middle East. Now open in the United Arab Emirates, Qatar and Kuwait, the emporium-like shops offer a similar experience to those in New York, including a salad station where customers create their own salads, daily-changing soups and home-baked pastries.

below | Dean & Deluca, Roppongi, Toyko designed by Wonderwall.
opposite | MPreis, Innsbruck designed by austrian architect Rainer Köberl.

MPreis

For many years, the Tyrolean supermarket chain MPreis has used architecture to distinguish its brand. As far-sighted as this practice may be, it is even more unusual, however, in that the company commissions new stores without insisting on a universal corporate look across its properties; instead, with each new project, it remains open to fresh architectural schemes. The SuperM in Telfs is a particularly sculptural design, like a gracefully squashed aluminium eight, that responds sanguinely to its dramatic alpine surroundings. The plan was to transform the traditional experience of shopping in a market hall into a more contemporary one. Backed up against the foot of a craggy mountain, the SuperM's backside features exposed grey concrete walls. The main facades are generously glazed, with windows up to six metres tall. The roof, clad with steel sheets, forms the long arc of a dragonfly wing, stacked atop another. The reason for the formal play of the roof is to serve as a sun-shade. Inside, the views onto the mountains and sky could be those of a world-class ski resort. As design increasingly becomes a strong differentiator of businesses, MPreis has had the foresight to recognize the SuperM's significance, and its ability to serve as an anchor of urban fabric, in an area that has been in the process of development.

above and below centre | MPreis supermarkets by peterlorenzateliers are distinguished by their unique architectural statements. The Telfs store exploits its striking alpine surroundings with vast walls of windows. Its unusual shape serves as a shade against the sun.
bottom left and far right | The Niederndorf store also features an unusual sun-shading system, using the slender trunks of birch trees to line the storefront, as if the whole market was tucked into a clearing within a forest.

Eataly

Introducing Turin to the world of small artisanal producers without the prohibitive prices, Eataly wants to make the finest food available to more than just a privileged few. In the brick-arcaded supermarket, shoppers can browse through Gragnano handmade fusilli, egg noodles from the Langhe, wine from the Veneto, oil pressed on the Ligurian coast, cured meats from Emilia and fish from the Bay of Biscay. The affordable prices are the result of paring down the distribution by taking out the middle man.

Cooking laboratories

Welcome to a new generation of spaces dedicated to the art of cooking. The dreary face of home economics classes that we remember from our school days is long gone. In its place are super-slick, brightly cheerful, mouth-watering interiors.

In her work with the ABC Cooking Studio in Japan, designer Emmanuelle Moureaux has created a whole new aesthetic for cooking schools. She eschews the steely utilitarian look of many cooking spaces in favour of glossy surfaces, bright blocks of colour and simple wood flooring. Moureaux has also designed a children's cooking school, with mini-Artek chairs, curvaceous counters and crescent-shaped tables.

The Tokyo Curry Lab restaurant by Kundo Koyama (famous for creating the Iron Chef TV show) is intended as a lab for experimenting with curry recipes and ingredients. Test tubes filled with spices line the interior, while the curvaceous dining counter and retro-futuristic moulded orange ceiling reinforce a sense of quasi-scientific experimentation.

Australian brand Little Kitchen runs a kids' cooking school out of its North Fitzroy retail store in Melbourne. The space features a custom-built kitchen designed especially for children, where they can learn basic cooking techniques and the joys of working with fresh organic produce.

from top | ABC Cooking School, Tokyo and ABC Cooking School for Kids, Kawaguchi by Emmanuelle Moureaux. **opposite** | ABC Cooking School, Tokyo, by Emmanuelle Moureaux.

Pudding Palaces

These spaces are dedicated to lovers of all things sweet and sugary. They include restaurants that serve only desserts and cafés where sweets are treated like dishes in themselves. The trend started in New York at the wonderful Magnolia Bakery, and we are now seeing the emergence of the Pudding Palace in trend-leading cities across the globe.

Martí Guixé, the food design innovator who also designed Camper stores, has now turned his attention to the world of candy with a new restaurant in Tokyo. The high-concept Candy Restaurant aims to formalise the act of eating sweets and raise it to the level of haute cuisine. Patrons can choose from one of four tasting menus. Each dish is then served with instructions, such as: '*Make sure you always eat a Fuzzy Peach with the stem side facing your tongue*'.

Also in Tokyo is the 100% Chocolate Café by Salon du Chocolat. Designed by Wonderwall, the café offers an array of chocolatey delights, from hot chocolate and pepper drinks to sweet sandwiches, classic desserts such as tiramisu and ice cream, and chocolate-covered amuse-bouches. The space is designed like a chocolate kitchen, with 56 varieties of chocolate displayed in sleek glass cases. Cocoa-coloured wood tables and chairs are complemented by ceiling panels which resemble a chocolate bar.

Architect Petar Miskovic has collaborated with conceptual artist Ivana Franke to produce Piece of Cake, a tiny bakery in Zagreb, Croatia. The space is shaped like a truncated pyramid and everything in the shop adheres to the principle of foreshortening perspective: less is more and things are not always as they seem.

---

from Top | The Tokyo Menu created by Martí Guixe.   **opposite from Top** | Chef at Candy Restaurant; Piece of Cake, Zagreb, designed by Ivana Franke and Petar Miskovic

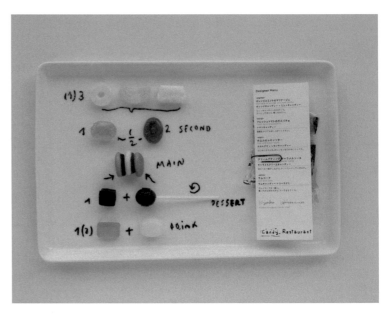

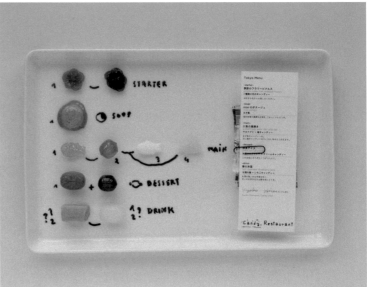

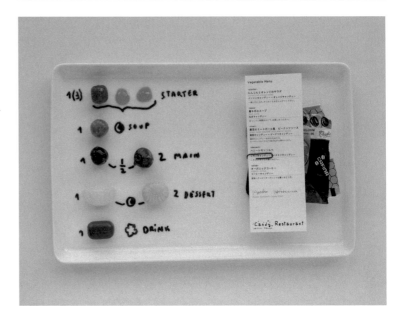

Luxe Canteen

As the trend for fast-moving gourmet food grows and temporary restaurants pop up in every city, canteen culture has at last gotten a grown-up look. These are hip places where friends and family dine and socialise. Warm and welcoming, Luxe Canteen spaces are designed to encourage conviviality and convenience, efficiency and elegance. Food and drink are served to share, and many of the dining spaces and areas are communal, open-plan, and designed to encourage the shared starter, or the collective pot or plate.

Long communal tables and retro school chairs evoke the hustle and bustle of a school dinner hall, while decorative wallpapers and statement lighting create an air of luxury. The interiors are modern, sleek and glossy, but contrasted with exposed walls and unfinished surfaces, ornate chandeliers and murals.

Dutch and Belgian café influences are to be found everywhere, such as Fabbrica in Rotterdam and Witloof in Maastricht. Also popular are do-it-yourself interiors, the presence of the objet trouvé, or workbench-like tables that nestle next to old-world bureaus, and cabinets or storage areas straight out of a no-nonsense East European workers' brasserie. The Luxe Canteen is often a conglomeration of stylistic elements assembled seemingly without rhyme or reason.

The latest London hotspot, Sake no Hana, has been designed by architect Kengo Kuma to resemble a traditional Japanese izakaya. The restaurant features informal dining at low tables and a menu made up of izakaya-style dishes in small portions meant to be shared. Bamboo, tatami, leather and black lacquerwork ensure this is authentic Nipponese canteen dining at its best.

In Stuttgart, Ippolito Fleitz adopted a Luxe Canteen aesthetic in order to recreate traditional Tuscan ideals of authenticity and homeliness at Trattoria Da Loretta. Diners sit at large wooden tables from the drawers of which they take their cutlery and napkins. Peter Ippolito explains that *communicative exchange is intended at Da Loretta, but not intimate togetherness*.

---

from top | Sake No Hana, London by Kengo Kuma + Associates; Trattoria da Loretta, Stuttgart, by Ippolito Fleitz Group. **opposite from top** | Amankora, Bhutan; Fabbrica, Rotterdam by Tjep; Amankora Gangtey, Aman resorts, Bhutan by Kerry Hill.

Bella Italia

At Stuttgart's Sicilian Bella Italia restaurant and wine shop, local architecture firm Ippolito Fleitz Group designed interiors in the spirit of a Renaissance Alice in Wonderland, lining ceilings and walls with more than 90 gilt-framed mirrors and circling tables with caned chairs in a spectrum of violet hues. Wine racks feature softly rounded corners while black-and-white photographs and white pendant lamps are clustered in homey profusion. Warm grey walls are complimented with classic dark wood furniture and, in one room, an unusual purple and mustard tartan wallpaper.

FOOD SPACES

La Terraza del Casino

Madrid restaurant La Terraza del Casino was redesigned in 2007 by Spaniard Jaime Hayon who has exuberantly modernized the Versailles aesthetic by playing with materials, finishes, scale and colour. Hayon simplified classical forms, turning fluting on a column sideways, adding amber coatings to the glass on French doors and draining the colour from classic quilted armchairs, leaving much of the furniture white or blue-grey. The high-gloss checkered floor has blue checks instead of black and squares of monumental diameter, matched by the diamond pattern of an entirely mirrored wall. Smoothing out ornament to its minimum while still preserving it, Hayon's inventive, hybrid and surreal environment is an match for chef Paco Roncero's innovative menus.

FOOD SPACES

Salon modern

After the theatrical, overt and showy nature of Nu Burlesque, we are seeing a rather more sophisticated, elegant and classical look emerging in the lounge, bar and restaurant sectors. This is very much in keeping with the current mood among consumers for a return to the old-world service ethos and a less hurried and 'process-driven' approach to hospitality. Even usually bustling bars are given a sense of ease and consideration, as at SBar in Los Angeles and The Artesian Bar, designed by David Collins Studio, at the Langham Hotel in London.

'As some of the more traditional establishments update their interiors, traditional styles are being revisited but mixed with modern touches and finishes,' says The Future Laboratory's Kate Franklin. *'This solidifies and focuses the revolt back to a new sense of tradition, for people who in many cases have no memory of how these things should be in the first instance.'*
Consequently, these venues mix classic pieces with modern juxtapositions of colour and material: bright turquoise leather provides a contemporary accent set against dark-stained wood furniture, while traditional damask and scroll motifs feature in Venetian style-cut mirrors, and stripes and small- scale chequerboard tiles add pattern and detail to floors.

Le Bar 228 at Le Meurice hotel in Paris is a prime example of the Salon Modern. Designer Philippe Starck has combined the original features of the room, such as panelled ceilings and frescoed walls, with his Dalí-inspired theme for the hotel to create a surreal but elegant space. Meanwhile, India Mahdavi's design for the Barclay Prime restaurant in Philadelphia combines updated classic elements such as dark, panelled walls and sleek wingback chairs with colonial touches like Ikat-print stools and animal hide rugs. The result is strongly graphic, yet warmly inviting.

These environments, then, need to inspire conversation and make guests feel special and relaxed in an atmosphere that is about a heightened sense of luxury and old-school glamour, especially effective in private dining rooms, such as those at the new Ivy Club. Attention to detail in the furnishings is therefore key: these are intimate spaces to relax and luxuriate in – only the best will do.

from top | S Bar, California, designed by Philippe Starck; Le Bar 228 at Le Meurice hotel, Paris, designed by Philippe Starck. **opposite from top |** Designed by David Collins Studio, Artesian Bar, Langham Hotel; Barclay Prime, Philadelphia, designed by India Mahdavi.

Silk Bed Restaurant

'*Hearing-Seeing-Tasting*' is the mantra of the Silk Bed Restaurant in Frankfurt am Main, which features 55 single seats or 'bed-places' and a room for a private group of 60 guests. Designed by German agency 3deluxe, the 208 square metre interior is a study in pink and white (even the oak floors are stained pink) with sheer curtains and delicate metal ornaments partitioning the dinner couches into eight sections, which are illuminated with changing coloured light. The cushions of each couch are illustrated with floral motifs rendered in Swarovski crystal. Guests to the Michelin-starred Silk are asked to arrive at the same time, exchange their shoes for slippers at the entrance and go back in time to an era when Romans reclined on couches to enjoy their meal. Chef Mario Lohninger offers an aperitif to ready guests for the following 10-course menu inspired by French, Asian and American cuisine and served on bespoke dishware.

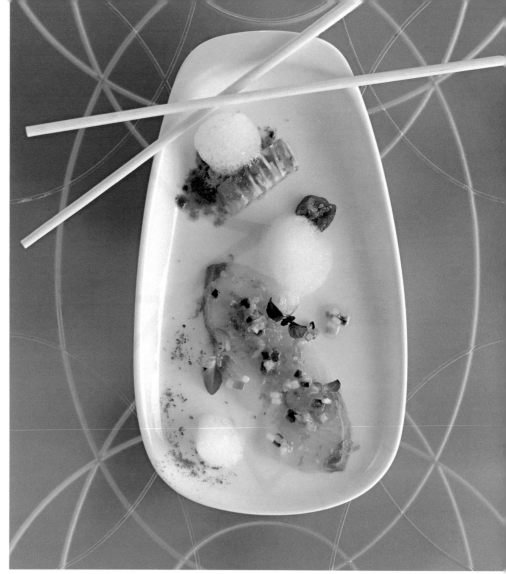

Maedaya

Black walls corseted with thick Manila rope (like traditional sake bottles), Melbourne's Maedaya Grill & Sake Bar was designed by local Architects EAT and demonstrates that using a banal (even salvaged) material does not mean sacrificing sophistication. The floor above, however, is stripped down to stainless steel, lacquered wood and bright-white walls. Equally modern, the interiors are a succinct illustration of the fact that the most modern aesthetics are not limited by material – somewhat akin to the food industry.

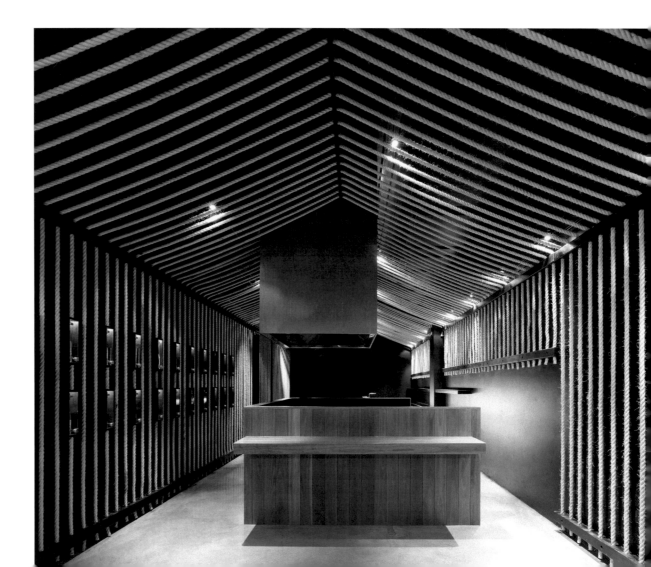

T-O12

Dedicated both to the country's first president, a bon vivant
named Theodor Heuss and to the revitalisation of its Stuttgart
neighbourhood, three-storey nightclub T-O12 by Ippolito Fleitz
Group and i_d Buero features a black and white interior, the
urban theme of which is played out over mirrored surfaces and
in dramatic white illustrations on walls and ceilings. The
surreal illustrations riff on the icons of street-life, including
street furniture, while the mirrors, reflecting pinpoint LED
lighting and rectangular white stools, make intimate lounges
feel spacious. Radiused white Corian bars feel like graphics
themselves. Images of insects and carnivorous plants typically
found in warm, dark places creep over the walls and ceiling of
the lower level. A staircase connecting the levels is marked up
with quotations from Theo himself.

Praq

Tapped to design a restaurant that would appeal to both adults and children that would avoid the worn tropes of the family eatery, Tjep. created the first Praq in Amersfoort and was followed by an additional location in 2008. The environment is dictated by its massive farm-style roof with thick exposed wooden beams. The designers created elements that served as both decorative objects and functional pieces: a table is also a window, a bus or a kitchen. A six-metre installation anchors the center of the room, resembling a colourful game of Connect Four, while providing a satisfying contrast with the handcrafted architectural elements.

Pluk

Haarlem-based take-out restaurant Pluk offers
fresh juices, yogurt shakes and salads. Pluk
offers the healthy food that should be consumed most of the time alongside the fun food
that should form less of our diet. Tjep. team's
interior design aims to communicate this
union of health and pleasure. The designers
placed faux fruits and vegetables into three
color groups along the counter by creating a
special gradient effect that took months to
develop. Even the colourful wall graphics of
produce seem to make the eyes hungry.

Yelo café

In the basement of the BHV store Belle Epine in Thiais, France, L'Annexe is 2,900 square metres dedicated to teenagers. Designed by Frenchwoman Matali Crasset, it is divided into four zones: agir (to act), s'évader (to escape), bouger (to move) and fashion. These zones are anchored by a 'platform' for eating and socialising called Café Yelo. Yelo, in powerful chartreuse and plum hues, serves pastas, milkshakes and vitamin-enriched smoothies at reasonable prices while hosting eclectic events, ranging from graphics displays, performances of dancing and music (it is surrounded by a raised platform for DJs) to capoeira demonstrations and African dance workshops. Yelo is organised around a 'court' with amorphously shaped bench seating that oozes at the foot of a thick central column where kids can lounge, recline, lean or sit astride seats to talk. Large, octagonal, barrel-like rings contain seating and tables for more intimate groups, circling the central column like an encampment. On one side, another octagonal structure with open panels, resembles a vendor's stall and sells groceries and, as Crasset phrases it, 'gustatory curiosities', including Japanese products. 'L'annexe operates according to a new logic,' Crasset explains, 'progressive, open to the exterior, and always changing according to the image of its young clientele.'

FOOD SPACES

clockwise from top left | The rear dining area partitioned by Dan Graham's Dividing Wall, perfect for spying on fellow diners, as well as the artwork that gave its name to the bar, a sign by artists Michael Elmgreen & Ingar Dragset; an area for lounging created by Ernesto Neto; water shoots out of the drain and hits the faucet in Massimo Bartolini's industrial sink-like Fountain; one of Olafur Eliasson's three lamps; Johannes Wohnseifer's My Night Is Your Day is a wall map on which the earth is delineated by vertical light cylinders that get light up and fade as the sun's position changes relative to the earth, tracking its rotation

Karriere

World-class art installations fill Karriere in the Flæsketorvet neighbourhood of Copenhagen, but it is not a gallery, it is a restaurant and bar. Olafur Eliasson has contributed three lights, the Local Career lamp, the National Career lamp and the International Career lamp. Dividing walls and room dividers are common in the public realm and in restaurants, but Dan Graham's Dividing Wall isn't sound-absorbent and opaque as most restaurants insist; instead, Graham's, set among outdoor café tables, is made of reflective, sheer, perforated steel and glass. Diners can listen through some panels and see through others, but they can't avoid their own reflection while eaves-dropping. Statuettes of the Virgin Mary and Adolf Hitler by Maurizio Cattelan populate rooms in the eatery while Kristoffer Akselbo's toaster burns the Mona Lisa into the morning toast. Robert Stadler, who straddles the worlds of art and design, has written poetry for the washroom mirrors consisting of puns and memorable sayings borrowed from his family and friends, like graffiti that anticipates its writers.

Flood

Mathieu Lehanneur's interior and furniture designs for Paris restaurant Flood attempt to match the quality of the international food with the quality of its air. To filter the space's air, Lehanneur placed an aquarium (above and opposite bottom) in the centre of each section of the interior that contains over 100 litres of Spirulina Platensis, or micro-algae. Through photosynthesis, the algae generates pure oxygen. He also created bespoke furniture based on the notion of flooding by dip-coating the PVC furniture and indicated the quality of the oxygen-enriched air via the blown-glass pendant lamps (below).

Living kitchens

As consumers become increasingly concerned about reducing food miles and bringing produce closer to home, designers are developing 'living kitchens', where herbs and vegetables can be grown – and even animals can be reared.

Alexandra Sten Jørgensen explores the concept of bringing produce closer to home in her Ethical Kitchen project. The kitchen recycles water and food waste to nourish a living plant with the caveat that, if not enough material is recycled, the plant will wilt.

German creative director Mike Meiré explores our relationship with food in the Farm Project, a walk-in installation for luxury kitchen and bathroom brand Dornbracht. Meiré brings the kitchen back to life in a refreshing move away from today's ubiquitous minimalist kitchen spaces. Pigs, lambs and chickens jostle for space alongside food and family, while pots and pans hanging from the ceiling create a busy, rustic feel.

Designers are using the kitchen as a medium for a dialogue on current issues of sustainability and ethics. Design consultancy PostlerFerguson presented "The Future on Your Plate," an exhibition that examined how the way we cook can demonstrate our attitudes towards the environment and the world's future. The project traced a line from global social and environmental changes to future domestic environments and cultural rituals associated with food. It examined the compromises that will have to be made in the face of a radically different future and the resulting positive possibilities. PostlerFerguson believes our relationship with food shapes our personal lives and our global environment via production, distribution, consumption and cooking.

from top | *The future on Your Plate'* project by Postler Ferguson examined how the way we cook can demonstrate our attitudes towards the environment and the world's future; *'The Farm Project'* by Dornbracht is an improvised living space filled with materials, animals, plants, and objects. it aims to create an antithesis to the minimalist design that has taken over the kitchen in recent years.
opposite from top | Detail from *'The future on your plate'* by Postler Ferguson Detail from The Farm Project by Dornbracht, The Ethical Kitchen by *'The Ethical Kitchen'* by Alexandra Sten Jørgensen encourages the perception that ethical living is no longer a matter of choice but a lifestyle we will all need to adjust to. Recycled water and food waste nourish living plants within the kitchen – if you don't recycle enough, the plant will wilt; detail from *'The future on your plate'* by Postler Ferguson.

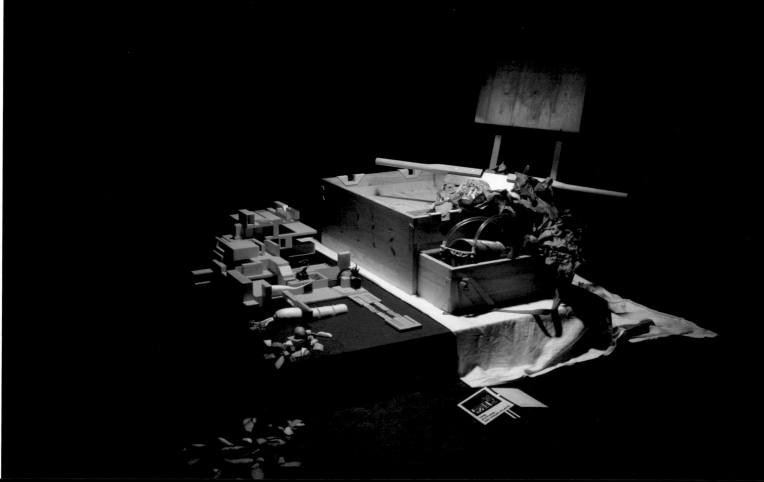

Bar Nestlé

The temporary Bar Nestlé designed by Swiss team Fulguro for the 40th Montreux Jazz Festival, was set on the shore of the city's lake. Inspired by paper boxes, like the packaging that chocolate comes in, Fulguro designed a platform to extend from the water's edge onto the water and terraced it in order to create the most generous view onto the landscape. On one side, a middle section of the roof opened to allow guests to order food and drink at the bar, as well as providing shelter during inclement weather. The structure was also designed to be rebuilt for two subsequent festivals.

Illy Push Button House

Espresso impresario Illy's Push Button House converts at the push of a button from a typical shipping container into a five-room home (including kitchen, dining room, bedroom, living room and library). Designed by architect Adam Kalkin, Push Button was intended to be as eco-friendly as it is practical: To this end, Kalkin constructed it from salvaged and recyclable materials.

TYPO /
LO /
GIES.

You are what you eat. And what you eat is increasingly defined by a complex set of views, attitudes and aesthetic cues that are difficult to define.

Dig into the nation's shopping baskets, fridges, cupboards and food diaries, and you reveal a unique snapshot of new consumer shopping and eating habits. For some, food is a means to a decidedly synthetic and vitamin-laced end, while others embrace food for its expressive and cultural potential as well as its nutritional content.

The future of food is not about numbers, but about emotions, passions and states of mind, as well as cupboard love and shopping basket lust. Anybody can cook up the figures, but to figure out what makes people cook up a storm in the kitchen, the information is in the detail: the Wall's sausages next to the Berocca, the caviar next to the fufu flour, the Duskin Farm pure English apple juice paired with the organic Fairtrade chocolate.

CREATE.

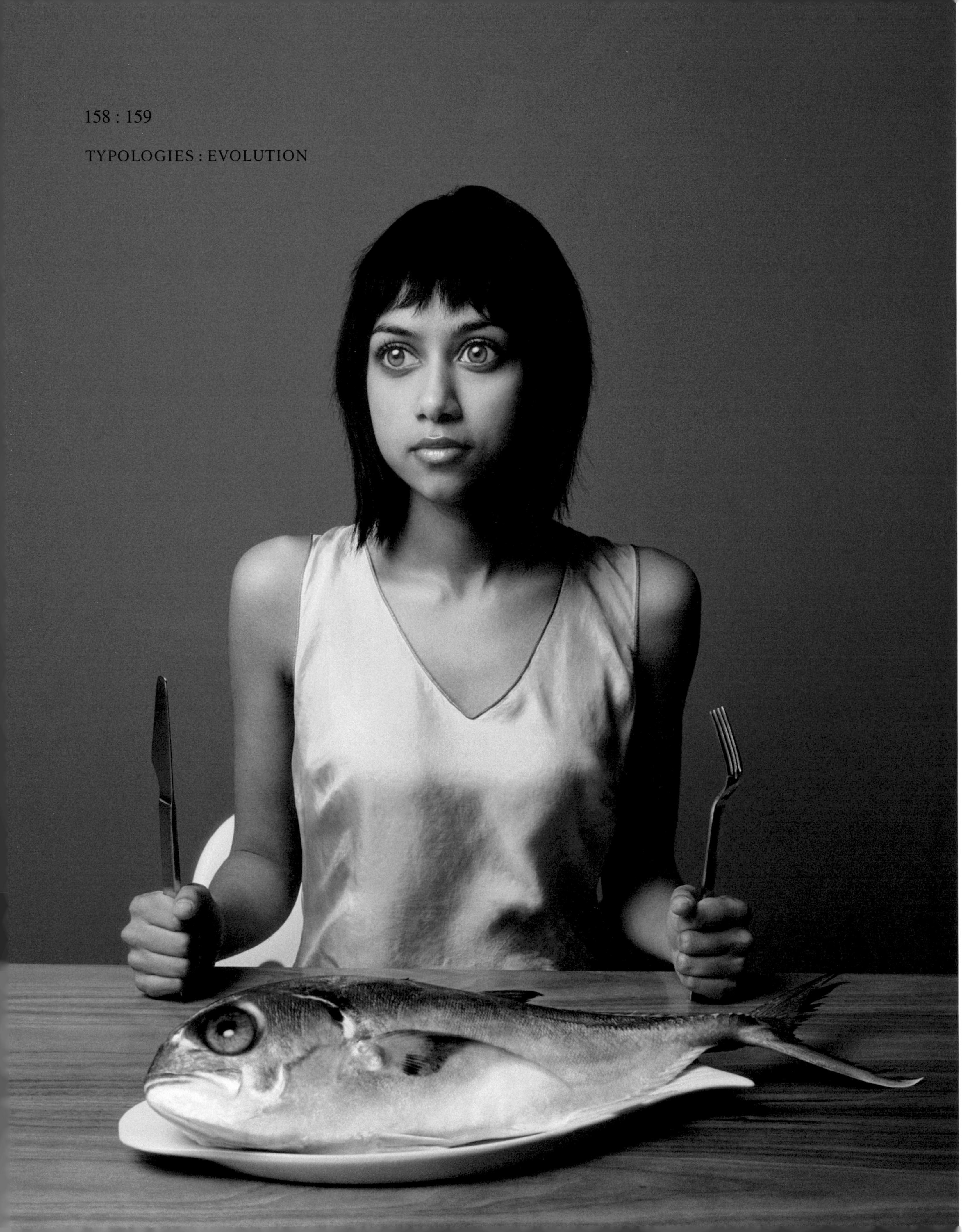

ZENO YOUTH

The debate about genetically modified food does not resonate with our Zeno Youth. Proudly urbanite and native to the digital world, Zeno Youths don't automatically equate organic with quality. After all, this is a generation that has grown up with the concepts of hybrid pets and successful cloning.

Tuck shop

Mainly found within the 16 to 24 age range, Zeno Youth is a niche group that has no holistic relationship with food. When Zeno Youths get hungry – which is often – they eat whatever they feel like. This is not to say that they live on junkfood. The media buzz over healthy living hasn't passed them by completely and they make the connection between health problems and eating too much fat, salt and sugar. However, their diet swings between healthy and unhealthy, including breakfast cereals, fried chicken, fish and chips, home-cooked vegetables and vitamin tablets.

Zeno Youth sees genetically modified crops as a way of ensuring that there is enough food for everyone, via crops that can resist drought, disease and pests. They have not thought about the potential complications because they see technological advances as a force for good. They represent an emerging wave of changing attitudes towards science.

Clone rangers

Similarly, if cloning animals can relieve food shortages and help breeds become disease-resistant, Zeno Youth has no qualms. This January, the US Food and Drug Administration gave its final go-ahead on the introduction of cloned meat into the food chain. Zeno Youth is unperturbed by the prospect.

Vitamin-enriched

For Zeno Youth, eating healthily is often about opting for a quick fix. If they eat fruit it will be pre-prepared and chilled, minus time-consuming natural elements such as seeds or skin. Zenos and those in need of a quick health top-up have pushed up the sales of chilled, prepared fruit radically in recent years. Zenos are also keen on enriched foods, from dairy produce with additional Omega-3 to vitamin-enriched juices and breads. The whole-food fanatic would see these as gimmicky, but the Zeno looks upon them as the perfect antidote to their synthetic food favourites and hedonistic lifestyles. As their name suggests, Zeno Youths are open to the idea of Zeno foods such as vitamin-enriched or vaccine-boosted produce. And they aren't wrong about this: Ingesting enriched products is one way of ensuring that the diet is rich in nutrients, vitamins and other healthy food components.

Genetic modification can also be used to battle disease. Yellow rice has already been genetically engineered to include vitamin A to tackle deficiency and the resulting blindness in parts of the developing world. Now extra lycopene is being added to tomatoes to fight prostate cancer. Zeno attitudes, which may seem extreme today will be shared tomorrow by a growing number of people who buy into the food science argument.

Live nodes

The Zeno Youths are constantly '*on*', in contact with their friends via online network sites such as Facebook and MySpace, microblogging using Twitter or Jaiku, even networking on the hoof with Bluetooth-enabled applications such as Cityware. They are deep in the wireless web, which suits their zippy attention spans; food rarely makes it onto the radar.

An interesting counter-trend to those at the leading edge of this movement is the tendency to just '*switch off*'. This does not mean an anti-technology attitude; it is about achieving tech/life balance. Zeno Youth George Stratton is one example. '*I unsubscribed from Facebook after I broke up with my girlfriend because I didn't want daily updates of what she was up to.*' This generation is in control of technology rather than consuming passively.

Nu cultures

Zeno Youths find their identity through involvement in subcultures. They are a part of the wacky racers who cycle round the city on customised fixed-gear bikes, battered from street slams and car collisions. On weekends they might get together for a spot of bike polo, the new hybrid sport taking over the Zenos' neighbourhood basketball court. They are the two-wheeled urban warriors and if bicycle lanes don't exist they'll either race along pavements or simply paint the lanes in themselves, as the Other/Official Urban Repair Squad (OURS, aka The Bike Squad) does in Toronto.

'I have a very different opinion about food than my mum. She gets a £12 box of organic vegetables from Riverford Organics every week, whereas me, I don't bother with organic or free range. She gets her brown rice and other bits from Marks and Spencer but I'm not really bothered where my food comes from. I'm vaguely conscious of food miles but to me the whole organic debate is just hypocritical. It uses more land to grow the crop and there's as yet no evidence to show that it's any better for you.

'I don't have a problem with pesticides. Firstly, there's no evidence to show that they harm the environment, and secondly, I'd much rather be eating something treated with chemicals that have been tried and tested for 20 years. I never wash apples before I eat them, for example. But with organic no one knows, and the crops are full of mycotoxins and bacteria.

'In terms of my diet, I eat a few portions of fruit and vegetables a day but I don't bother trying to eat five. Sometimes I'm healthy, but other days not so. I'll have fast food when it suits me and just take what I'm given at work. I'm a nurse and the food on the ward centres around bought-in, pre-prepared products like powdered mash or packaged chocolate cakes. I'm fine with that, I see it as fuel. I think, it's here, it's free, I might as well just eat it.

'It's good because I save money by eating at work and I would sooner eat really cheaply if it means I have more money for going out. If I'm skint, I'll borrow food off my flatmates, or grab fast food when I'm out and hungry. Having enough cash to spend on the gigs and disco nights that I go to is more important.'

---

from left | Cheestrings Light is a quick and easy snack with an appealing synthetic texture; E Boost Daily Health Booster claims to activate energy, immunity, recovery and focus; Berocca multivitamin and mineral supplement contains essential nutrients to aid a hectic lifestyle.

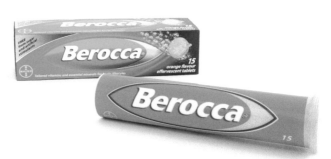

EXTREME CONNOISSEURS

The more obscure the ingredients, the more complex the cooking process, the more fulfilling the dining experience for the Extreme Connoisseurs. For these super-foodies, life is about the pursuit of the most extraordinary eating experiences for both kudos and personal fulfilment.

Status symbols

Generally, in the ThirtyfiveUp range (experience-driven, grown-up Generation Xers), these individuals have been married to their work for most of their lives and are now in a position, financially and in terms of seniority at work, to begin devoting more of their time to interests and hobbies that fulfil and challenge them. Also, they have already acquired all the trappings of material wealth – car, house, watch, wardrobe – and are looking for new arenas in which to explore and flex their financial muscle.

The menaissance

Extreme Connoisseurs are predominately male. According to food writer and trend consultant Kevin Gould, cooking is an indicator of virility. *'Cooking involves rhythm and science, and gives men a chance to display connoisseurship,'* says Gould. *'It's interesting that there are few female wine connoisseurs. And the few there are care primarily about taste and flavour, not the acidity of the soil and all the things that boring male wine buffs seem to be obsessed with. It's exactly the same with men and kitchens.'*

They are extremely concerned with quality and authenticity and have considered growing their own produce, but for the Extreme Connoisseur it's not about an allotment. If they have moved out to the country, then a vegetable and herb garden is par for the course, but for the urban dwellers, weekly shops are conducted at specialist luxury delis and organic food suppliers.

Culinary expeditions

This is the most adventurous of the food typologies – there is nothing that they won't try. Ortolan (an endangered bird, which is force-fed before being plucked, drowned in cognac and eaten whole) and the Japanese fugu pufferfish (the internal organs of which are lethal and must be prepared by a licensed chef) have both been on the menu for the Extreme Connoisseur. They take intense pleasure in tasting the bizarre delicacies of the places they visit. *'Travel and food are very much linked,'* explains Stefan Gates, author of Gastronaut. 'Both are about discovering the new, about being enriched and should be educational.

Hi-tech home

Extreme Connoisseurs are bringing professional cooking techniques into their home. The most likely consumers to go for specialist kitchen appliances such as teppanyaki plates and planchas in their homes, they have also become interested in home sous vide units. *'Sous vide'*, literally *'under vacuum'* in French, is a method used by chefs such as Grant Achatz of Alinea, Chicago, Ferran Adrià of El Bulli, Spain and Pierre Gagnaire of the eponymous Paris restaurant. Food is cooked and then vacuum-sealed in a bag before being slowly cooked in a water bath with meticulous attention to times and temperatures. This gentle cooking process is thought to produce tender textures and more intense flavours.

Into the wild

Environmental concerns around food miles and seasonality are encouraging the British consumer to enter even more adventurous food territories. Today the UK is home to as many as 50 professional foragers, each with several hundreds working for them. Trawling woodland and nature reserves for road kill and wild fruits and vegetables, they then sell to top London restaurants such as the Ivy, J Sheekey, Moro and St John. The British palate is changing and the Extreme Connoisseur is happy not only to eat but also to participate in supplying that palate.

Extreme Connoisseurs are going for game such as venison not only because it provides new alternatives but also for health reasons: venison is virtually fat free. These are the people who are leading the shift towards eating more game, including venison, rabbit and pheasant.

---

below from left | Vintage Nr. 1 is brewed by the Jacobsen Brewhouse in Denmark. A barley wine, 10.5% alcohol, it is aged in Swedish and French oak casks for six months. Only 600 bottles have been produced and these cost 2008 Kroner (around 200£) each; Prunier caviar recognised as a market leader with 'expertise in choosing'grading and importing the finest caviar from producers on the Caspian Sea'; Venezuelan Black is made from 100% cacao 'The finest, rarest, most expensive cacao in the world'.

CASE STUDY | Sam Chatterton Dickson
40, a director of Angela Flowers Gallery plc, London

'I will never order steak in a restaurant, it's as common as muck and I can cook a better one myself. For me eating out is about trying something new. I'll try sheep's testicles or sheep's heart, or anything that I haven't heard of before.

'I've developed a bit of a reputation amongst my friends for eating the strange stuff, so I have to live up to that. I ate chicken feet the other night, offered them to my flatmates who, as usual, turned the offer down. Chicken feet aren't my favourite thing; I wouldn't, for example, choose them to be my desert island dish, but I like to eat them because it gives me a way into Chinese culture. It's a way of seeing what makes the Chinese tick. With chicken feet and lots of Chinese cuisine it's about textures as much as flavour.

'In my mind, I think if a person can eat it, then I am open to trying it. It seems hypocritical to me to eat the leg of an animal and not eat the heart. Why eat flesh and not muscle? By that same token, if you eat eel then why wouldn't you eat snake? If you eat it when it's dead, then why not eat it when it's alive? I would try a beating snake's heart for these reasons, I would be very anxious and I can't say I would enjoy it but I would try nonetheless.

'I started out as a student eating Findus Crispy Pancakes but gradually moved up the culinary ladder to kedgeree and spaghetti bolognese and now cooking and entertaining is a really important part of my life. I am careful about where I source my ingredients and do splash out on really good quality meat and fish. I wouldn't class myself as a showy cook, although I do have the stainless steel towers so I can pile up different ingredients on the plate and it does look really good. Usually it's one-pot cooking and I don't shock my guests too much; I would serve them the risotto I made from my garden snails.'

CREATE.

FOOD THRIFTS

Food Thrifts use food as a metaphor for how they want to live their lives. Their focus is shifting away from material trappings, with cooking becoming the latest in cultural capital. They are a varied bunch, ranging in age, income and occupation – more so than any other food consumer type – but they share a deep knowledge of food and understanding of quality. They feel passionately about food shopping, dining out and cooking for friends, and pride themselves on their culinary fluency.

Culinary upbringing

It is likely that Food Thrifts have been brought up in a household where the emphasis was on quality, homemade cuisine. So, despite a 300% rise in consumption of ready meals over the past decade, they have stayed true to their principles. Food Thrifts prioritise cooking from scratch and opt for restaurant or homemade food at lunchtime in lieu of the run-of-the-mill office sandwich. Even for the younger, less wealthy members of this category, the quest for high-quality food sends them to high-quality markets and are in the habit of buying top-quality produce.

Mature consumerism and redefining value

There is a shift of emphasis for the more mature Food Thrifts in their 30s to 60s, who are likely to have reached their personal goals of style and wealth. They are now focused on improving and enjoying their quality of life by 'trading up' on essentials such as food, rather than amassing more belongings. Food Thrifts notably choose to spend most money on food items that will improve the quality of the whole meal, such as luxury olive oil or butcher-bought meat. There is an emphasis on simple but perfect ingredients.

This shift towards simplicity also means that consumers are starting to see the value in paying premium prices for essentials. Because the era of cheap food is coming to an end, the Food Thrift is pioneering the move towards more discerning consumption. For all Food Thrifts, quality not quantity is what's important. One member of the LifeSigns Network, who works at a gourmet food distributor on a graduate wage, says: '*I'd rather eat a good steak once a fortnight than beefburgers every night.*' Despite budget or demographic, a wholehearted Food Thrift will always pursue quality.

Thrifts believe in rewarding themselves by eating quality food. One explained that he eats a gastro-pub lunch every day, despite working as an unpaid intern, because he '*deserves it*' and it is the '*highlight of his day*'. Most Food Thrifts tend to have a sound level of self-esteem, and those who don't might use thriftiness as a healthier, albeit more expensive, alternative to comfort eating. Generally though, people in this group respect their bodies and their health, hence their willingness to spend lavishly on their fuel.

The weekly shop

Food Thrifts shop at stores like Whole Foods Market and pick up extras from specialist food stores, farmers' markets and the local greengrocer. They have the food intelligence to recognise quality and will happily mix the finest imported ingredients with local herbs and vegetables from their neighbourhood Turkish grocer. This group have supported the rising number of specialist food shops and delicatessens. Food Thrifts have also inspired supermarkets to go upmarket, extend their ranges of luxury foods and launch premium labels.

---

clockwise from top left | Daylesford organic Scottish smoked salmon; Rick Stein pickled ginger from his Specialist Ingredients product range; Arroz SOS spanish rice; Herb saver by Prepara prolongs the life of your fresh herbs by up to three weeks; Carluccio's balsamic vinegar.

'We never had a microwave at home when I was growing up, Mum made everything from scratch and I've carried that on. I never buy anything packaged. It just doesn't make sense. First, you can save a whole load of money if you make it for yourself and secondly, it just doesn't taste as good. I never buy tomato sauce, for example, I'll always make that myself. It's also because I love cooking, it's my creative outlet.

'I take food pretty seriously, it's an important part of my life. I like to feel that I'm eating well, which means investing in good ingredients and taking my time with the eating and the cooking. I still take care to be moderate, what I eat is a mix of bog-standard stuff from the supermarket, like tinned chickpeas or lentils, and then a few choice ingredients.

'Not everything has to be pricey. I usually find I spend quite a lot on meat or fish from the local butcher or farmers' market because I know it will be worth it. Once you've splashed out on one really good item, other bits like the vegetables don't need to be so refined. For me, it's more about the aesthetic of cooking. I like to work with ingredients that look good, are interesting, colourful and fresh, they don't have to cost the earth.

'I definitely have a weak spot for cured meats like salami or chorizo, but I justify splurging on those when I'm at the market because I don't fritter money away in other parts of my life. I have a nice flat, I am interested in fashion but food is where I really get passionate. I can potter around supermarkets, little grocers or street markets for hours and spend most of my weekends doing something food-related: shopping, cooking or eating.'

ARMCHAIR EXPLORERS

These ordinary people are willing to experiment and have left the couch to spend more time at restaurants and in the kitchen, using technology to concoct or connect to a wide range of foods.

Armchair Explorers shop at the supermarket once a week, but this is supplemented with weekend or evening trips to local butchers, fish markets and specialist ethnic supermarkets for that special occasion which could equally be a dinner party or a night in with a DVD. The fact that members of this group are heading to specialist shops and ethnic supermarkets in their downtime tells us they regard home cooking as a leisure activity and are hungry for global food knowledge. Ethnic food means big business in some areas.

Hometainment

These are average earners who are working their way up the ladder. One of the key trends amongst this group has been the rise of 'hometainment': staying in rather than going out. Food now plays a bigger part in their home and social lives and the way they spend their free time. In the past, they might have scrimped on or avoided the weekly supermarket shop, especially if they are male. Now this has become an enjoyable experience, which partners or flatmates share and turn into weekend expeditions.

Endangered dishes

In some places, classic dishes are facing extinction because the ordinary palate is branching out to ethnic cuisines, trading shepherd's pie or meatloaf for Thai, Mexican or Moroccan, and the Armchair Explorer is blazing the trail. An interest in all things foreign means traditional dishes just don't cut it any more.

Food television

This group relates to food television. They tune in to the new wave of cookery shows where youthful, entertaining presenters encourage them to have a go and bend the rules. Their interest has also been aroused by non-food elements in these shows, such as an attractive host, a celebrity or a political agenda. While Jamie Oliver goes off to save the chickens, 'MasterChef', with its combination of culinary skill and hard-edged competition, is sparking interest from the Armchair Explorers and getting them into the kitchen, keen to outdo the show's contestants and treat their mates. The show has been a ratings hit: the recent final in February 2008 peaked at 5.7m viewers, wiping the floor with other channel rivals.

Takeaway gourmet

Armchair Explorers still have a lazy streak and regularly order in takeaways or purchase convenience meals. However, traditional orders are being replaced by ethnic and lighter cuisine, starting with Thai. Armchair Explorers are partly responsible for the rise in fast-moving gourmet foods, which they order from the Internet or using their mobile phones.

Gastroblogging

Armchair Explorers have been integral to the gastroblogging craze. They click onto popular sites such as Chez Pim and Chocolate & Zucchini to document their kitchen adventures, exchange recipes and pick up tips from the down-to-earth citizen critics. Some try their luck at the more professional sites such as Chadzilla where enthusiasts flex their molecular gastronomic savvy.

Nu flavours

The Armchair Explorer prides himself on his knowledge of global foodstuffs and feels quite the master in the ethnic supermarket. The market now needs to respond to his taste for global flavours, which are branching out from Indian and Thai into new territories such as Japanese or Jamaican.

---

from left | Walkerswood spicy jerk barbecue sauce; Levi Roots Reggae jerk BBQ sauce for authentic Jamaican dishes; Bombay Authentic Madras luxury curry sauce; Brindisa Pulses, *'For authentic Spanish and modern European dishes'*.

'My tastes are really wide – there's no excuse for not having that in this day and age. Globalisation has brought everything to us so our palates should be broad. For me, food is about ideas, people and mixed cultures. I like the global stories behind food and I like to try new cuisines.

'I eat a lot of Jamaican, Pakistani, Iranian, southeast Asian and Turkish cuisine and I'm learning more all the time. I learn when I go shopping for food because I visit the little grocers, I like to see what different cultures eat. When it's mango season from May to July, I'll buy a box of mangoes a week, if durian is in, I may splash out on that, I spent £20 on a durian last week.

'I like hunting down funny ingredients like cola nut. When I asked for that in the African grocers, I surprised people, they were wondering how I know about it. I also recently bought the Ethiopian bread, injera. I don't really know much about Ethiopian cooking yet, but I'm going to learn. I'll visit the restaurants, chat to some of my Ethiopian friends and give it a go.

'I get inspired by shopping, travelling and also TV, I really enjoyed MasterChef. That's the thing about cooking and it's what I think the show highlights: someone can be ugly or fat or whatever, but put them in a kitchen and their cooking can still amaze you, it stands up for itself.

'I do of course fancy myself as a bit of a master chef. I don't get stressed or rude in the kitchen, not at all, but I really pay attention to the flavours and I try to recreate art on the plate, I look at contrasts of sweet and salty or soft and chewy. When it comes to the kit, that's all really important too, I will easily pay three figures for a knife. Steelware and copper-bottomed pots, a good whetstone and grinders for coffee and herbs are all really essential parts of my kitchen.'

ETHICAL EATER

For the Ethical Eater, food is a political issue. Ethical Eaters were early adopters of Fairtrade, organic and locally produced foods, and these remain the essence of their diet. Price is the only barrier that would restrict such foods from making up their entire menu.

Moral pursuits

Ethical Eaters are part of a growing number of consumers who are civically minded, socially motivated and environmentally aware in their shopping habits and purchases. The move towards ethical eating has been the most important change in the food industry in the past 20 years. For these 'conscience consumers' their credit cards are ballot cards. By handing over their cash to a specific brand they are saying that they know and trust its ethical practices, share its politics and expect a portion of its profits to benefit consumers and worthy causes.

The Ethical Eater is usually a student or in his or her late 30s or 40s. They tend to be low to middle-range earners in industries which interest them personally, such as care work, the environment or academia. Their career path has often been surprisingly varied, and they have experimented until they've found work that really means something to them. These knowledge-seekers often become mature students and are the least likely consumer type to work purely for financial gain.

Ethical Eaters might also be found in dull but relatively stress-free nine-to-five office jobs or part-time work, which doesn't impinge on their hobbies and interests. These interests, such as singing in a choir, practicing yoga, tending an allotment or keeping up with current affairs, are usually community-spirited.

Healthy roots

Ethical Eaters are sensible, healthy, no-nonsense eaters. They consumed healthy foods such as brown rice and soya milk before these became readily available, which shows a certain rebellious, independent attitude to media messages and mass-market tastes, and a willingness to take control of their diet and seek out the exact foods they want. Ethical Eaters are beyond food fads and diets; for them, food is firmly about healthy eating and has been so for most of their lives. As a result of fear, uncertainty and doubt, the mood created by war and political uncertainty, health is now their primary concern.

Reading the label

Ethical Eaters shop at major supermarkets once a week, filling their trolleys with organic and Fairtrade products, alongside special offers as they are budget-conscious. They tend to shop relatively slowly, checking labels for nasty chemicals, and 'editing' the supermarket's mass-market offer. Today's consumers are hungry for information.

First, they campaigned for nutritional value to be detailed on packaging; now, according to figures released from Mintel in February 2008, 84% of adults also want the recycling credentials of packaging to be listed.

Ethical Eaters are well-educated and can knowledgeably discuss issues such as globalisation, modern religion and politics; they surround themselves with like-minded people they can learn from. They probably read their local paper rather than a national and purchase niche or specialist magazines such as Ideal Home, The Ecologist or Ethical Consumer. They will not support charities they don't believe are socially responsible. Green charities such as Friends of the Earth are their favourite causes.

Trading fair

The quest to take control of the shopping basket is on. Ethical Eaters try to ensure all their fruit and vegetables are organic or Fairtrade and are urging supermarkets to be proactive too. According to Fairtrade Labelling Organizations (FLO) International, global consumer spending on Fairtrade products topped £1bn in 2006.

Going local

To varying degrees, the Ethical Eater tends to be anti-capitalist. This is one of the reasons they try to buy food from local sources and individuals rather than from corporations. They form part of the Localvore movement, which supports food from local producers.

---

from left | Apple juice from Duskin Farm, a small family farm near Canterbury, Kent. Owners Andrew and Jenny Helbling started making apple juice over twenty-five years ago; Honest Tea products are USDA organic certified, high in antioxidants and low in calories; Organic marmalade from Bunalun who aim *'to bring you simple, everyday essentials before they are 'improved' and dulled by laboratories and factories'*; Rachel's organic natural bio-live yogurt made from organic wholemilk; Marks & Spencer organic Fairtrade milk chocolate.

Charlotte Onslow
30, programme manager, Gender Action for Peace and Security

'Food is not just about fuel for me, it's something I consume in a cerebral way. I'm acutely aware of international geo-politics because of what I do and I pick and choose my food boycotts depending on what's going on in the world. I didn't buy any produce from Israel, for example, during their recent war with Lebanon. There are brands that I avoid, like Nestlé. I haven't touched a KitKat in over ten years.

'I grew up on a farm, and it formed part of my conscience. It's simple, food comes from things and convenience, packaged food that you can't touch just doesn't do it for me. When I was young, being called out to dig up some potatoes for dinner just wasn't cool and I was embarrassed about it, but now I realise it's good that produce really comes from the ground.

'For me, it's about getting control over your life. I'm into slow food that takes time to grow and time to prepare. I cycle everywhere so I don't have to rely on public transport. It's also why I do yoga, it gets you back into contact with your body and through that you gain control over it. I also love to read, that's a form of entertainment that you really have control over, you decide when you do it, how fast you do it and when you want to reflect back over it.

'My consumption of food is also based on the idea of community and locality. I'm thrilled that I now have a milkman, Kevin, and we have our little chats. It's much better than the checkout girl down at the local Co-op who never acknowledges me no matter how many times I go in there.

'I also grow what I can at home and use my own chillies, tomatoes, aubergines, lettuce, rocket, lemons and all manner of herbs. I do have a distant pipe dream that I will one day have chickens and freshly laid eggs in the morning but not at the moment. I'm definitely too urban to go live just yet.'

CULTURAL CHASERS

Many second-generation Asians and Africans, are in a unique position from whence they can draw on two sets of cultural heritage and two sets of culinary history and tradition.

Kitchen tales

Cultural Chasers have grown up eating the traditional food of their parents, and foods that may seem exotic to their friends are standard fare for them. They will be familiar with asafoetida, amala flour, tamarind, garam flour and cassava from being sent out on shopping missions by their parents. They can be quite picky about eating out at restaurants that serve food from the '*motherland*' and many Cultural Chasers are unforgiving of restaurants that serve food that bears no resemblance to the home cooking they are used to.

Finding the right takeaway

Britain's appetite for ethnic cuisine is high: according to research from Startupsplus, the marketing service for catering industry suppliers, of all the restaurants opened last year, 40% served ethnic food ranging from Persian to Japanese, Kurdish, Nepalese and Korean. While these new options thrill the Armchair Explorer, the Cultural Chaser is less easily pleased. '*I don't just go to any old Indian,*' says a LifeSigns Network member whose origins are in southern India. '*In fact, there are only three restaurants in London that I deem of a high enough standard to order from.*'

Perhaps these high standards are why our Cultural Chasers aren't usually competent at cooking this food for themselves. Once they leave home, they are likely to get their jerk chicken or saag paneer from the local takeaway - one they know and trust - rather than make it themselves. This is due to lack of time. Ethnic cooking techniques can take a long time to perfect; for generations weaned on instant gratification this isn't an attractive prospect.

Mash-up generation

'*Authentic Indian food consists of recipes that have no precise measurements and were traditionally passed down verbally through the generations, perfected by spending years practising at your mother's side,*' says Vicky Bhogal, author of Cooking Like Mummyji, a cookbook aimed at Cultural Chasers. '*Second-generation Indians have greater social freedoms, academic aspirations and career goals, all of which mean that the time-consuming method of learning how to cook these much-loved dishes is becoming impractical.*'

Cultural Chasers are proud of their heritage but often identify more with their adopted nation's values, as this is the environment where they have grown up. The 25-35 age group is the furthest removed from their parents' culture. Conservatism is eschewed for nights out on the tiles and shopping sprees. This demographic prefers dining out, ready meals or instant Western solutions. However, they are aware that there is a wealth of culinary heritage they have not yet tapped into. For some, this

awareness is slowly being mobilised, and they are making an effort to pay more attention around the family home. For others, there's a feeling that they have a whole life ahead of them to learn Mama's tricks.

Mash-up culture and the cut-and-paste ethos that frame the lives of the New Millennials suit the young Cultural Chaser perfectly. Borrowing ideas and trends from different cultures to create a concept that is uniquely personal is an important goal for these groups, and this is exactly what the Chaser does every day. They comfortably reference the music, style and fashion of Asian, African and West Indian cultures. They love movies such as 'Third World Cop' and 'Monsoon Wedding', which offer real insight into life in their parent countries. As they still live at home, they are likely to help their parents at dinnertime, making rice or other simple dishes and gaining an introduction to cooking methods.

CASE STUDY | Kat Wong
Kat Wong
30, Radio 1 producer

'I absolutely loved school dinners. Bread and butter pudding, shepherd's pie, all those British classics, it was the cuisine that I never got to taste at home. School lunches leave me with fond memories because as a kid they opened me up to both worlds, Chinese and English. My father ran a Chinese restaurant, so food always played a massive role in my life and that of my family. As kids, we would stay up late for midnight feasts fresh from the restaurant: roasted duck, spring rolls and noodles. We always ate Chinese at home unless my mother was preparing her version of spaghetti Bolognese or pork chops, which was never quite right, everything always came with rice and a fried egg.

'Today, cheese is a large part of my diet but I can remember a time when my brother and I had just never tried it. I had my first taste when I was about 16, and I turned to him and tentatively said: 'Shall we try it?' Back then it was just a bog-standard cheddar but we decided we liked it and, at that point, we hadn't even discovered the cheese grater. Then the fun really began. Now my parents always buy me a cheese board for Christmas, only no one else eats it but me. For me, cheese is like a culture, it has grown with me, as my taste gets more refined and takes on the more complex varieties.

'I've also honed my skill at making a Sunday roast, only I used to do those on Mondays, my day off. My boyfriend at the time and I used to call it 50s Mondays, because I would slave over the meal for hours. I like to try to cook the food of wherever I am. When I was in the States it was all about making meatloaf, on my recent trip to Italy I made a point of learning how to do a good pizza. With Chinese cooking it's always been more complicated. It's something that I have never tried to recreate in my home, probably because I feel that it will never be as good as what I was brought up on. When I want Chinese food I go home for it, but I do want to learn the techniques myself now. It's been on my mind for the last few years and I'm finally doing something about it.'

clockwise from left | Oil made from hemp seed. Grown in north Devon by Good Oil; Miss Khoo's Asian Deli Essential Curry powder; Tilda steamed pure basmati rice.

FUTURE SOLU\ TIONS.

Expect the following emerging trends – touching on everything from food (from scratch or ready-prepared), its packaging and the environments we eat in to the tools we use to construct our meal or with which we eat it, even our kitchen and shopping spaces – to begin to hold sway over mainstream consumer tastes in the coming five years. With these central categories, we can begin to see a picture of how the future of food looks and the ways we may want to respond to it – emotionally and aesthetically.

| Euro Vase by Hana Vítková, 2007.

GRANNY MODE

Granny Mode embraces our desire for authenticity, with an added helping of nostalgia for kitchen memories that many of us may never have actually had. Certain foods recall a post-war period where rationing was balanced by wholesome fare and flavoursome treats. As a trend, Granny Mode lives not just in the past but offers a contemporary reworking of old-fashioned ideas with balance at its centre: high fat and small portions, simple food packed with flavour, leftovers with ethical twists and functional practicality with pretty and homely decoration. Here we see traditional colours and patterns updated with modern finishes and treatments: Robert Dawson contemporising iconic Wedgwood patterns, the return of teapots, tea services and jugs, and traditional Pyrex.

The terms
/ *Culture = mother*
/ *Eat with integrity*
/ *Waste not, want not*
/ *Seasonal approach*
/ *Heart of the home*
/ *Pleasure & family*
/ *No nonsense*

The colours
/ *Rose pink*
/ *Post-war pastels*
/ *Mixing-bowl brown*
/ *Wooden spoon*
/ *Cherry red*

The designers
/ *Labour and Wait*
/ *David Mellor*
/ *Ineke Hans*
/ *Hella Jongerius*

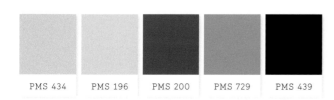

| PMS 434 | PMS 196 | PMS 200 | PMS 729 | PMS 439 |

opposite from top | Ladle Set by Labour and Wait; Brown Betty teapot by Labour and Wait; pie from Canteen restaurant. **clockwise from top left |** j'ai oublié la nappe vintage cider bottle; Craft pottery, a hand-thrown and wood-fired collection of stoneware pots by John Leach Potter; Chérie, vintage baking tray by Lara Ferroni; Traditional Scales, Cast Iron, Brass Scoop by David Mellor; Raapsteeltje en andere verhalen Good food project Designed by Simone Kroon, Photographed by José van Riele; a white and red tiles tablecloth designed by 5.5 designers and manufactured by Bisazza; japanese wicker bowl from Conran shop.

Witches Kitchen

For Artecnica, 40-year-old Netherlands-born, France-based Tord Boontje created the sustainable ceramic cookware and wooden utensils that he imagined would fill a witch's kitchen and kit out her bag of tricks. The utensils, including a pair of salad tossers shaped like a hag's hands, in addition to a variety of double-ended serving forks and spoons and a dagger-shaped knife, were hand-carved by Guatemalan artisans from locally harvested, sustainable and reforested wood. The ceramics were formed by hand by Colombian potters who draw on a centuries-old ceramics technique, which allows them to embellish the surfaces with the textural impressions of leaves.

CONVIVIALITY

Luxe canteens, from the shared tables at Amankora, the luxury Aman resorts dotted around Bhutan, to the dining room at Shoreditch House, mark the trend towards arenas in which the principal activity around eating is no longer seeing and being seen, but talking and engaging with fellow diners. Conviviality moves from being bright and optimistic to warm and intimately lit. Shared dishes and pots are now an accepted aspect of dining as restaurant goers move away from three- or four-course standards. Rolling dishes delivered in a steady flow change the dynamic of the eating experience, making it more informal, less staged and more intimate. Within the home, this translates into simple and straightforward food preparation, with a minimum of time spent on fussing and maximum time spent on talking and quaffing. This can range from Jamie Oliver's approach of bunging oil-drizzled tomatoes in the oven to the repackaging of micro-ready rice.

The terms
/ *Eating is living is sharing is life*
/ *Long wooden tables and benches*
/ *Corner seating*
/ *Food as leisure*
/ *Regional Chinese*
/ *Rural Italian*
/ *Bowls and pots rather than plates*

The colours
/ *Honey*
/ *Stone*
/ *Crimson red*
/ *Lacquer*
/ *Washed grey*
/ *Worn wood*

The designers and manufacturers
/ *Droog*
/ *Maurice Mentjens*
/ *StudioIlse*
/ *Martino Gamper*
/ *Naoto Fukasawa*

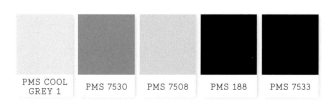

PMS COOL GREY 1	PMS 7530	PMS 7508	PMS 188	PMS 7533

opposite from top | Kacheltafel by Reiner Bosch gives homeliness a sleek industrial look. Photography Vincent van Gurp; Rip and Dip by Sebastiano Oddi; Carry on Collection by Mater. **clockwise from top left |** Total Trattoria by Martino Gamper at The Aram Gallery brings people together in a dining experience supported by design; carafe by Kiki van Eijk; Salad servers by John Pawson, When Objects Work; Warm Gift designed by Tonfisk; black ceramic bowl by Conran Shop; Artek Bambu collection; Shoreditch house dining room designed by Tom Dixon; Dumpling kitchen by Jin won Hee encourages diners to share and engage with their food in a more intimate experience.

Sharpen Those Taste Buds

Tokyo industrial designer, Oki Sato's Nendo collaborated with local patisserie owner Tsujiguchi Hironobu, the brains behind popular sweets shops like Mont St. Claire and Le Chocolat de H. Following a number of conversations between Sato and Tsujiguchi, the candy king developed an original dessert inspired by Nendo while Nendo created new tableware for Tsujiguchi's chocolate shops. Sato created his fluted white dishes with the intention of displaying the beauty of each of his friend's confections like a painting on a canvas. The result of these dialogues was the 'chocolate pencils,' which come in a variety of cocoa blends in differing degrees of intensity. Diners can use the accompanying pencil sharpener to grate chocolate shavings onto their dessert. Usually leftover shavings go into the trash as one sharpens a pencil – in this case, they become a delicacy.

The Future Kitchen

You may well ask: What will a small kitchen look like in 10 years? Designed by Antoine Lebrun for Fagor Brandt in order to identify, highlight and envision the technological and social trends that will affect the look and operation of our kitchens. Lebrun's multifunctional kitchen unites electromechanical and vegetable technologies and takes advantage of plants developed by aerospace industry. As users cook, these plants serve as a filtering and ventilating hood while providing a renewable supply of clean water and vegetable soap. After the meal, dirtied dishes can be placed in the sink and, with the hood closed, receive a genuinely green scrubbing. Aion filters polluted water, odors in the air and generates a soapy substance. A reaction to population and urban growth and the increase in living costs and insecurity, as well as an accompanying shrinking of personal space, Aion offers multiple functions in one piece of furniture and brings the outside indoors, raising the quality of life.

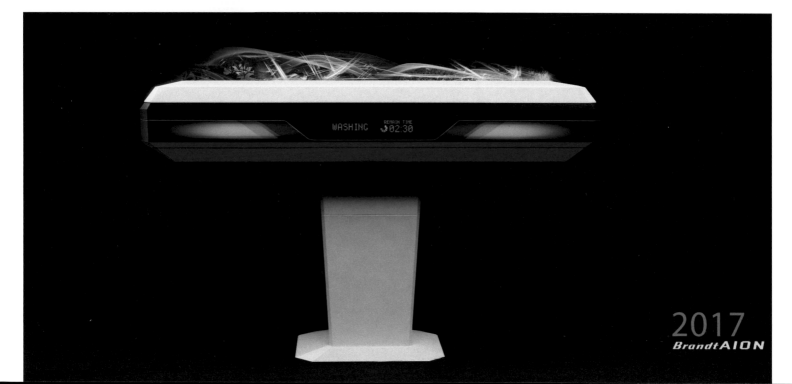

2017
Brandt AION

FUTURE SOLUTIONS

SYNTH CULTURE

'Embrace innovation' is the mantra of the Synth foodie. This group sees food more as fuel than a pleasure or social interaction, often relegated to on-the-go consumption. The trend treats food like a tool in a tool-kit that enables other more important activities. Everything here is about collaborating and meshing, rather than creating an identity that is unique. Pop and Nu Wave brights translate into vivid, ergonomic furniture and environments by designers such as Karim Rashid, where futuristic shapes and colours emphasise optimism around the artificial and the desire to synthesise. Bold packaging and shapes, new graphics and fonts, innovative developments and hi-shine finishes are key.

The terms
| *Neon brights*
| *Teflon finishes*
| *Innovation*
| *Bendy materials*
| *Irreverent design*
| *Fun product*
| *High shine*
| *Graphic pattern*

The designers and manufacturers

| *Karim Rashid*
| *Wonderwall*
| *Art and Cook*
| *Normann Copenhagen*

The colours
| *Candy pink*
| *Lime green*
| *Yellow*
| *Fuchsia*
| *Ultramarine*
| *Bright violet*
| *Turquoise*
| *Ice white*
| *Fluoro orange*

| PMS 396 | PMS 225 | PMS 164 | PMS 3125 | PMS 2607 |

opposite from top | Bleeding paint chair by Anna Ter Haar;
Bauer Bar, Tröstau, Germany; Jensen bowl by Normann
Copenhagen. **clockwise from top left |** Anan Japanese
noodle bar designed by Hosoya Schaefer for Autostadt;
Playful bunny and carrot kitchen roll holder by Alessi; Metal
skin table by Peter Marigold; Green tea set by Chris Misiak;
Astro Bar, Reykjavik designed by Michael Young; Vitamin
water in all-important bold packaging; Majik Cafe, Serbia
by Karim Rashid. The room is equipped with screens that
broadcast SMS text messages onto screens in the lounge.

FUTURE SOLUTIONS

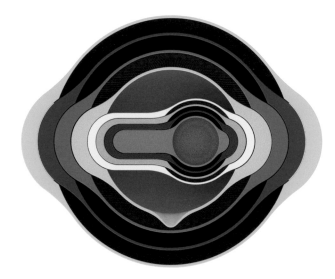

Return to Ornament

Nest 8 mixing bowls, colander and measuring spoons and cups by Morph UK for Joseph Joseph are a vivid example of the kitchen's return to colour in recent years, from appliances to dishware. But colour is only one symptom of a larger embrace of ornament that includes everything from more baroque dishware patterns to exquisitely complex forms on the handles of cutlery and serving utensils.

Rotterdam-based photographer and designer Elise Rijnberg wove her The Art of a Table Setting tablecloth with a nearly textbook illustration of how to set a table for casual or even formal occasions and which cutlery, glass or plate corresponds to which course, in effect, recounting for diners a narrative about western food culture and etiquette. Even crystal stemware by Demelza Hill is given an extra flourish that marks each piece in a mismatched collection of glasses as family to the others.

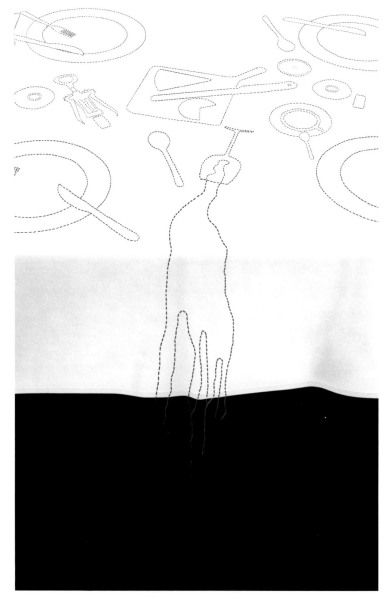

opposite top | Nest 8 Stacked, rendered by Morph. opposite below | New Lease of Life by Demelza Hill. right | MESSY tablecloth, designed by AZE design.
below from left | Demelza Hill's Snap and Dine is a single use three-course table setting that integrates disposable cutlery with traditional silverware. The portable lunch setting expands the possibilities of eating outdoors in style whilst reinforcing the correct use of cutlery, which has been lost over time. This is achieved through the decorative qualities and formal setting which both are a visual reference to fine dining. This product is fun and interactive whilst raising the standards of current eating on the go habits; The Art of a Table Setting by Elise Rijnberg.

FUTURE SOLUTIONS

SHAPING FOODS

The revival of craftsmanship is happening throughout the design industry, without skipping over the food industry. Artisanal foods are finding new acceptance and an elaborate response in the fantastical realm of sweets.

Making Out With Marzipan

The Eugene and Louise Bakery is inhabited by monsters of the sweetest kind, the creatures of Glenn D'Hondt and Sylvia Meert (aka Eugene and Louise) and Tinne Mermans. Made laboriously from marzipan, they include the eternally open-mouthed Bobo (bottom left), a very upright looking fellow with blue hair named Jeremy (top left), and the frowning, four-legged and emphatically exclamatory Tweak! (top right). The Dead Clown, whose trepanned head hinges gaily open, is friends with The One and Only Marzipan King (below), who lives beneath a slender glass dome. Graphics for the bakery reflect the owners' prolific inventiveness, with illustrations of the toothy marzipan monsters gracing postcards (middle) and chocolate wrappers, alike. For an exhibition in Antwerp, E&L displayed a smooth white marzipan hand in a bureau drawer (below right), the remains of the tragic romance of the gallant Prince Arthur: As soon as Arthur placed a sugary token of his love on the white chocolate finger of his beloved Princess Sweetheart she melted away in his arms, leaving him with nothing but her scrumptious hand. If visitors find the stories at E&L to be a bit dark, it's probably because they're made from chocolate.

Sugar, Water and Glucose

Papabubble was first established in Barcelona in 2003 by Tommy Tang and partner Crick as an artisanal caramels shop, where all the sweets are handmade from sugar, water and glucose in flavors that range from grapefruit and pear to raspberry and cinnamon. Today, there are Papabubble outposts in Amsterdam, Tokyo, New York and Seoul, where about four batches of lollies and hard candies can be produced by each pair of workers daily. After the sugar mixture is boiled, it is poured onto sheets to cool into malleable puddles. To change the colour of the material, a worker may stretch sheer taffy-like ropes of it repeatedly over a hook, drawing air into the mixture to render it opaque. Depending on the nature of the sweet, it may need to be pressed with spatulas, pulled, grafted onto different coloured ropes, coiled, rolled, cut with scissors or molded (using a cookie cutter-like tin) from sheets of cooled sugar that resemble stained glass and then placed in clear bags and jars. And most fun of all, bespoke requests from customers are happily brought to life.

FUTURE SOLUTIONS

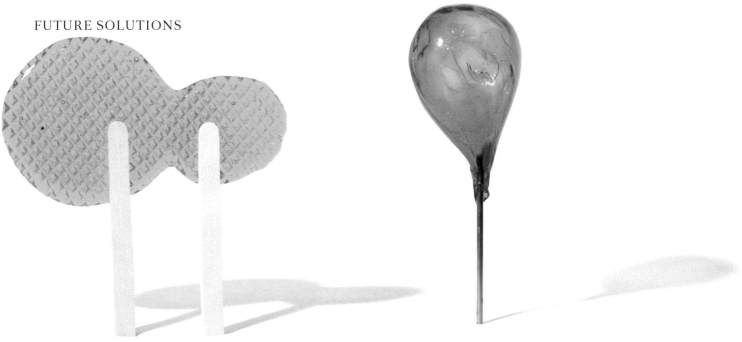

this page clockwise from above | Sébastien Cordoleani and Franck Fontana for Papabubble sweet store; candy hearted tree in autum; Papabubble Barcelona front store; the sweetest cow on earth.

CHEW (SLOWLY) ON THIS

Chewing thoroughly and eating slowly has always been a good mum's advice but designers today are suggesting we also take the time to reconsider the value of our food.

Think Twice

Inna Alesina's prototype canvas and wood produce bag has individual compartments to make shopping for fruits and vegetables a considered and thought-provoking experience. Ukrainian-born, Baltimore-based Inna Alesina is the principal of Alesina Design Inc., a product design and development studio, focusing on universal and environmental design. The pockets of the produce bag store and display produce as something precious in opposition to brown or plastic shopping bags into which groceries are typically shoved without thought and with great haste.

right | WANT - NEED. The small hole divides the volume of the glass into two parts: 'need' (below the hole) and 'want' (above the hole). Please be careful while filling the glass and cover the hole with your thumb while drinking, thus you can stop the waste (in the global sense) with your own hands. Want/need glass is a humorous souvenir that addresses a serious problem. below | Produce bag has individual compartments to make shopping for fruits and vegetables a special experience.

HEALTHY EATING

Functional eating and added benefits appeal across age ranges, from the eat-anything teen to the looks-obsessed Baby Boomer. Healthy means clean, modern and active, and packaging and design need to reflect this rather than a 'whole earth' aesthetic. Information is paramount as the consumer wants to know it all, to feel both informed and in control. Words and graphics factor highly and delivering knowledge becomes the integral aesthetic. Strong, primary colours dominate, with traffic light oranges and greens signalling simple messages. Transparent packaging allows an honest approach and encourages direct relationships.

The terms
/ *Clean*
/ *Functional*
/ *Active*
/ *Immediate*
/ *Rapid return*
/ *Perceivable benefit*
/ *Transparency*
/ *Optimum*

The designers
Alessi
Tjep.
Philippe Starck
Peter Marigold

The colours
/ *Warm orange*
/ *Grass green*
/ *Black*
/ *Carmine red*
/ *Slate grey*
/ *Lime green*

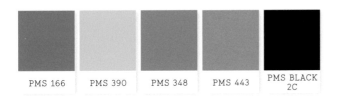

| PMS 166 | PMS 390 | PMS 348 | PMS 443 | PMS BLACK 2C |

opposite from top | Tesco's venture into the U.S. takes the form of *'Fresh&Easy'* by Coley Porter Bell. Clever branding signifies health and environmental benefits; Peter Marigold screw-in cutlery for raw vegetables; Marks & Spencer low-calorie *'Count on Us'* ready meals; Munchy seeds also uses this primary colour story to endorse the health benefits of its products; Les Menus bébé baby food.

clockwise from top left | Nat Restaurant in Hamburg uses only regionally sourced ingredients; Wild Bunch & Co make only 100% organic juices, which can be taken in a shot in one of their organic shot bars; 3poäng floor lamp by Macmeier; Marks & Spencer eat well range; Liz Chair by Kartell; Hovis Seed Sensations designed by Jones Knowles Ritchie uses clear packaging and traffic cone colours; Tesco's Healthy Living range by Coley Porter Bell, Dr Yes Chairs by Kartell.

INTO THE RAW

The austerity aesthetic of the post-war period has been re-invented for the authenticity-obsessed and ethical shopper. Matter and meaning combine to create products where the look and feel has to be married to concern for current hot topics such as food miles, carbon footprint and sustainability. Local overtakes organic as a prime concern, and value for money means that high prices will be stomached if the expense can be rationalised as simple, honest, real and true. Avoid fuss, frills and the over-modern – it's all about stripping back, paring down and revealing rather than adding. Scrubbed wood comes together with pewter effects for the return of the traditional inn, a place where expressions like 'honest fare' dominate. Hand-written packaging meets natural materials and uncomplicated shapes. All this represents rural simplicity for the time-poor urbanite, who will happily devote hours to home-grown vegetables, which end up more expensive than anything to be found at Fauchon.

The terms
| *Honest and basic*
| *Simple and natural*
| *Down to earth*
| *Uncoated*
| *Oak*
| *Cardboard*
| *Localvores*

The colours
| *Brown tones*
| *Warm greys*
| *Greengage*
| *Duck-egg blue*
| *Ochre*
| *Black*
| *Chalk white*
| *Seaweed*

The designers and manufacturers
| *Piet Hein Eek*
| *Conran*
| *Matthew Hilton*
| *E15*

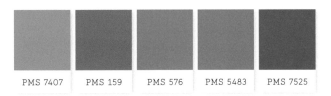

| PMS 7407 | PMS 159 | PMS 576 | PMS 5483 | PMS 7525 |

opposite from top | Madame Lilli table and Backenzhan stool designed by Philip Mainzer for E15; First Blush Alcohol-free juices share wine's flavour and antioxidants. **clockwise from top left |** Red Sugar Superfood Café in Edinburgh by Space Solutions and photographed by Simon J Hollington; wooden salad bowl in The Conran Shop 'outdoor living' collection; Michael Young was commissioned by Base Design and Passanha oil to design this new glass bottle for the re-launch of this historical olive oil company; Organic sand white dinner plate in The Conran Shop 'outdoor living' collection; Thomas Eyck's new collection 'Woven Willow' designed by Stefan Scholten & Carole Baijings; ringfin dining chair by Matthew Hilton for De la Espada.

The New Authenticity

Hamburg-based gastronomes love their Mutterland. The retro-modern supermarket, established by Jan Schawe, is marked by a handsome rusticity: dark wood crates, old white tiles and thickly-woven baskets at the bakery counter where the market's name is embossed in letters that look handwritten across the floury crust of bread loaves. The homemade jam and house-brand coffee are popular, along with slow food ingredients, traditional German favourites, local potatoes and wines.

Mutterland is a fine illustration of the fact that the austerity aesthetic of the post-war period has been re-invented for those who are looking for authenticity and ethical living. The updated look and feel of places like it and products that are made by foodies of like mind reflect a world view in which local takes precedence over organic, and value for money means that high

prices will be tolerated if the the item being purchased is perceived to have the values of simplicity and honesty. It also derives in part from today's concerns about food miles, carbon footprint and sustainability.

This is a style and a mindset that avoids fuss, frills and the overly modern – it's all about stripping back, paring down and excavating rather than adding on. Scrubbed wood is combined with pewter recalling the traditional inn, a place where expressions like 'honest fare' dominate. Handwritten packaging uses natural materials and uncomplicated shapes. All this represents rural unpretention for the time-poor urbanite, who will happily devote hours to home-grown vegetables, the care of which will sometimes end up proving more expensive than anything bought off the shelves of a gourmet market.

I/
N/
DE/
X.

EATING, DESIGN AND FUTURE FOOD

crEATe.

EATING, DESIGN AND FUTURE FOOD

crEATe.

_The content of this book is based upon extensive research done by The Future Laboratory on '*Future Food*' developments.

Gestalten has edited and extended their research to publish this sourcebook.

crEATe.
EATING, DESIGN AND FUTURE FOOD

For The Future Laboratory

Editor in Chief: *Martin Raymond*, Creative Director: *Chris Sanderson*,
Editor: *Gwyneth Holland*, Design editor: *Caroline Till*, Writers: *Sarah Bentley, Priyanka Kanse,
Gina Lovett, Sudi Piggot* and *Miriam Rayman*, Picture research: *Sophie Ekwe-Bell*

For this publication

Editors: *Robert Klanten, Sven Ehmann, Shonquis Moreno, Floyd Schulze, Ole Wagner,
Martin Raymond* and *Chris Sanderson*
Cover and Layout: *Floyd Schulze* for Gestalten
Typefaces: Romain BP by *François Rappo*
Generell TW: *Mika Mischler;* Foundry: *www.gestalten.com/fonts*
Cover Photography: *Ted Sabarese*

Project management: *Elisabeth Honerla* for Gestalten
Production management: *Janine Milstrey* for Gestalten
Proofreading: *Pat Mehnert*
Printed by *SIA Livonia*
Made in Europe

Published by Gestalten, Berlin 2008
ISBN 978-3-89955-231-7

For more information, please check www.gestalten.com

Bibliographic information published by the Deutsche Nationalbibliothek.
The Deutsche Nationalbibliothek lists this publication in the Deutsche Nationalbibliografie;
detailed bibliographic data is available on the internet at http://dnb.d-nb.de.

This book was printed according to the internationally accepted FSC standards for
environmental protection, which specify requirements for an environmental management system.

Gestalten is a climate neutral company and so are our products. We collaborate with the non-profit carbon offset
provider myclimate (www.myclimate.org) to neutralize the company's carbon footprint produced through our
worldwide business activities by investing in projects that reduce CO_2 emissions (www.gestalten.com/myclimate).